I first met Marina Kurban at Revival School in Te Anau, New Zealand. When I first heard her story, I was totally amazed that she not only survived her childhood but had become a confident, victorious over-comer during that process. *Love to the Rescue* is a gripping tale of her personal walk and how God's intervention saved her from destruction. The Lord literally plucked her up out of a miry pit and placed her feet on the mountaintop so that everyone everywhere could see that He was her Father and she was His child.

Today, Marina is one of the most shining examples I know of the Love of God. Her relationship with Him is exemplary, having been transformed into an instrument of light that is truly amazing! When she sent her story to me, I could hardly put it down. This book should be on the 'must read' list of every Christian, especially of those who are unaware of the tragedies that happen to children around the world who live under the shadow of addictions, poverty and lack. Thank you, Marina, for one of the most inspiring stories I know of.

— **Nancy Coen**
Founder, *Global Ascension Network*

I have known Marina since 2018 and have accompanied her on two trips to her project in Central Asia. Over the years, she has shared glimpses of her life story with me, but reading this book has only deepened my admiration for her strength and determination. Marina defies expec-tations, pursuing her dreams with unwavering resolve, no matter the cost. Her ambition, generosity, love, and compassion for her family and others never cease to amaze me—you would never guess the depth of trauma she has endured. Marina's story is a powerful reminder to never stop chasing our dreams, no matter the obstacles.

— **Amy Northcott**
Friend and Elder, *Wanaka Lighthouse Church*

I have known Marina as a congregant in my Messianic synagogue and have always appreciated her warmth, joy, servant heart, and worshipful spirit. Marina is a beautiful young woman within and without, and was a GREAT asset to our congregation. We grieved when she moved to New Zealand.

Reading Marina's history and after all the trauma she experienced, it is amazing that she has no physical or emotional scars evident. The transformative experience she had with the love of G-d in Messiah explains who she is. I am grateful that she has walked in that love and healing.

I highly recommend this book to anyone who has experienced family dysfunction or trauma, or who wants to learn about it. It will lift your heart as well as educate your mind and make the blessings we have in America seem all the greater.

— **Shmuel Wolkenfeld**
Rabbi, *Or HaOlam Messianic Synagogue*
OrHaOlam.com

What sparks and then sustains a dream to bring righteousness to a broken community? In *Love to the Rescue,* Marina relates her journey, with touching personal traumas, from a dysfunctional family in the depths of depravity, through the roller-coaster of life that touches normality, then spirals down to a low ebb, before rising again. With her innate sense of righteousness, Marina leads us to the present, where her hopes may be fulfilled. For anyone who doubts God's unconditional love and transforming power, this book clearly demonstrates His Lordship.

— **Edward Hutchison**
Senior Pastor (Retired), *Tapanui New Life Church*

I first met Marina in 2015. Benji Alexander had heard Marina speak in Gore and subsequently invited her to join us in Te Anau at Revival School. Since then, we have had a lot to do with Marina and her journey. If you asked me prior to reading this book whether I had heard Marina's story, I would have said yes. Wow, we didn't know half of it! When I started to read, I thought it sounded like a crazy work of horror from some degraded mind.

Marina's story is a brutally honest revelation of the depths of human darkness . . . from her firsthand experience. The suffering and horror that was inflicted on a young Marina is being mirrored in countless lives of children and youth today. Be prepared to see into the life of a child who has truly lived in darkness. But also be prepared to receive the hope that the transformational power of the love of God—not fiction, not imagined, but the beautiful power of an encounter with God's grace and love, and the power of God's light over darkness—has to bring beauty from ashes. To meet the Marina of today is to meet an amazing mum, a woman of unconditional love and light, and one who plunges back fearlessly into the darkness to save others. Be prepared to meet an actual Wonder Woman!

— **John Steffens MNZM**
Richmond New Life Church

The first time I met Marina I literally felt and saw a 'breaker anointing' on her life to free humans from the hell of past and present unresolved trauma and conflict. She doesn't just carry a 'breaker anointing' but she is willing to take it to the humans still living in the fields of human conflict, suffering, and travail. Without reservation, I endorse her and this book knowing she will inspire and share keys to help others break through instead of stay broken down.

— **Apostle Norm McLeod**
House of Breakthrough Churches Intl.

Several times while reading, I glanced up at my own children—tears in my eyes—taking a deep breath in the midst of the utter heartbreak and pain of Marina's story. I felt blessed beyond measure to see my children playing happily, healthy, with full bellies, and far removed from the burdens that Marina, her family, and her friends have had to endure—burdens no one should ever have to bear.

Marina's life story and her transparent brokenness serve as a canvas displaying the unconditional love and grace of God. I was moved toward the heart of the Father for those in similarly desperate situations—to rescue the helpless, to pray for them, to provide for them, and to do whatever I can to help. It is a striking reminder that, but for the grace of God, it could be me or my daughters in their place.

Marina offers a way to join this urgent fight. 'Invest in a Life' is a powerful and valuable opportunity to do just that, and I pray you will seek God's leading on what part you can play as your heart breaks for the many Allas, Galinas, and Marinas in the world.

— **Alanna Alexander**
Friend, NZ

This is a riveting action-adventure epic where the not-yet-hero, terrified, without succor and awash in despair, discovers and hones her superpowers; a saga of global perspective in which the reader strains with the hero to overcome, and from thence to dominate the Enemy of wholeness with the unmatchable weapons of Love. I am abruptly torn from the harrowing storytelling itself when I recognize the slice of her life where we first intersected. I vividly recall reading the pain and the inner struggle written on her soul back then. Today, however, I can see her wielding the Power of Love.

— **Shay Weber**
Friend, USA

С первых дней нашего знакомства Марина казалась необычайно взрослой и зрелой. Борьба и ответственность за жизнь сделала ее уязвимой и, не по возрасту, сильной. То, о чём пишет Марина в книге, не просто опыт, это одна из граней борьбы женщины за её судьбу от Бога. Так много страданий вокруг, иногда ты понимаешь, как слаб и несостоятелен ты, чтобы что-то изменить. Но пример этой девушки: спасая одного, ты спасаешь мир. За каждой жизнью — целый мир. Как удивителен Бог, насколько велика Его любовь, которая так отражается и прославляется в этой жизни. И какое чудо Божьей благодати — быть причастным к тому, что делает Он!

From the very first days of our acquaintance, Marina seemed exceptionally mature and grown-up. The struggles and responsibilities of life made her both vulnerable and strong beyond her years. What Marina writes about in her book is not just experience—it is one facet of a woman's struggle for her God-given destiny.

There is so much suffering around us that at times, you realize how weak and incapable you are of changing anything. But the lesson and example of her childhood is that by saving one life, you save the world. Behind every life, there is an entire world.

How wonderful God is, how great His love is, as He is glorified and revealed in Marina's life. And what a miracle of His grace it is to be a part of what He is doing!

— **Larisa Musayelyan**
Marina's foster mum and former Director, *Helping Hand*
Khujand, Tajikistan
Pastor and Head, *Tender Care*
(a healing and recovery project for church leadership)
Kiev, Ukraine

This story will tug on your heart, as time after time the odds of survival seem low—that is, until Marina encounters the love of GOD in and through people. *Love to the Rescue* is a story of the metamorphosis and transformational processes that have allowed her to emerge as a beautiful butterfly. I personally endorse this biography and believe with all my heart that many who are trapped in sexual exploitation or hard places will seek help in many of the ways Marina has done.

I am grateful to be friends with Marina and believe many will be touched by her amazing, heartfelt story. May Marina's hopes and dreams for world holistic centres become a reality!

— **Evangelist Owen Pomana**
(currently serving Ukraine)

I have walked alongside Marina for over a decade, partnering with her in anti-human trafficking efforts across multiple countries. I've heard her testimony more times than I can count—but from the very first page of this book, the full weight of what God has done in her life came alive in a whole new way.

The storytelling is masterful, woven together with such depth and clarity. The magnitude of the adversity Marina has faced—the crushing pain, injustice, and tragedy—is staggering. And yet, even greater is the enormity of God's grace and favor on one lost girl.

This true story left me in awe of God's goodness and relentless love for "the least of these."

Ultimately, God gets all the glory, as His supernatural and unyielding love captures Marina's wild heart. This book gripped my heart like never before.

— **Benji Alexander**
Founder, *Raising Royalty*

We will never forget the day Marina moved into our home in Khudjand in Tajikistan. The fragile teenage girl embraced the love of an ordinary Christian family with such an appetite. Unfortunately, the time we had together was brutally aborted by the civil war and us being forced to run from the country. Now, to read her story all these years later makes the tears flow. The book is amazingly written and so touching. It gives hope that Jesus can meet any broken heart with healing and restoration. We have always said that this girl is a fighter. The story of the book proves that. Warmly recommended.

— **Kari and Rune Borgsö**
Pastor, Heart Sthlm

In loving memory of
Athanasia Stephanie May Koutsimanis—my friend.

Your light touched everyone around you, and even though you're no longer here, the kindness you shared continues to ripple through this world. You brought so much love, beauty, and joy into my life. This book is for you—a way to honour the incredible soul you are. You are missed beyond words but loved beyond measure.

LOVE TO
THE RESCUE

TORN CURTAIN PUBLISHING
Auckland, New Zealand
www.torncurtainpublishing.com

ISBN Softcover 978-1-991299-59-8
ISBN ePub 978-1-991299-60-4

Typeset in Yeseva One, Ralway and Minion

Cataloging in Publishing Data
  Title: Love to the Rescue
  Author: Marina Kurban
  Subjects: Tajikistan, Russia, Norway, United States, New Zealand, Christian
    Memoir, Inspirational, Not for Profit, Human Trafficking, Global Missions,
    Child Exploitation

A copy of this title is held at the National Library of New Zealand.

LOVE TO THE
RESCUE

MARINA KURBAN

FOREWORD

AS A COUNSELOR, AUTHOR AND TEACHER IN THERAPEUTIC STUDIES, I read with great interest my student and friend's account of the trauma and trials of her early years in the chaos of Tajikistan's social upheavals and ensuing poverty. As I absorbed her recounting of those harsh years, it felt as if I was hearing again the prophetic voice of Rachel weeping for her children—and the cry to "turn the hearts of the parents to their children."

The compassion and love that can only come from the furnaces of suffering, humiliation, powerlessness and persecution are clear to see and marvel at in Marina's account of her traumatic childhood. Truly "those who are forgiven much, love much", and "God's strength can be most clearly seen in our weakness."

As I read, I witnessed again what Papa God can do and is doing with just one deeply bruised person who is yielded to His will as well as for those who would team up with her—for we too are sure that God's work, when done God's way, will not lack God's supply.

As a counselor, I gained new insight into the places of despair and desperation that are so often born of governmental and economic mismanagement and its ensuing poverty, combined with a sobering view of the enslavement of men to their sexual appetites and the consequential sexual enslavement of the most vulnerable—the women and children of poverty.

Love to the Rescue is certainly not an easy read, but it is deeply soul and conscience-stirring, enabling readers a greater realization that we are all called to remember the words of the Lord's own prayer, "May thy will be done on earth"—through Marina and Ryan, through you, and through me—"as it is in heaven."

I commend the charity 'Invest in a Life' to all whose heart moves them to partner with Marina and Ryan in their worthy cause.

— **David Riddell**
B.Th, PG Dip, Dip Grad.
School Dean
Living Wisdom Life & Counseling Skills International

CONTENTS

PROLOGUE

O N HER DAILY WALKS THROUGH THE CITY OF KHUJAND, A WIDOW in her late seventies noticed a young Crimean woman and her four daughters sitting in front of the grand Russian Orthodox church, begging. Today she decided to stop, though not to offer the destitute woman money or food. For a while now, Mina had been searching for a housekeeper. Seeing the scars on the young woman's body, Mina concluded that she, like so many others in her city, had decided that life on the streets was preferable to living with a brutal husband. For a fleeting moment, the older woman pitied the four children who huddled beside their mother, but she shook it off. *The older ones could be useful around the house. And a strong young woman might be able to bring in some extra income.*

The young woman looked up as Mina approached the steps. It had been a long day. Alla's work at the factory took all her concentration, yet it still wasn't enough to provide a roof over their heads for her and her children. She held out her hand, hoping at least for enough rubles to buy her daughters some bread. When the woman in front of her offered her and her children lodgings in exchange for house help, she didn't think twice. *Food and lodging in exchange for doing an old woman's menial household tasks?* The moment Mina proposed the arrangement, Alla gestured to the children and began following the old woman home.

Most days, the older children helped their mother with the work of cleaning Mina's house, cooking the food, and taking care of the laundry. Then, leaving the younger ones in the care of their older siblings, Alla would head back to the factory where she spent her days at the seamstresses' table. The hours were long, but she was satisfied. Most of her meagre income went to Mina, but maybe one day she would be able to afford to rent an apartment for herself and her children. For now, at least, they were safe.

◆ ◆ ◆

ONE EVENING, AS SHE MADE HER WAY HOME FROM WORK, ALLA pulled her scarf closer around her ears. A cold northeasterly wind blew over the rugged foothills of the Pamir Mountain range, whipping around the city buildings and rushing through the streets of Khujand. Relieved to be finally home, she trudged up the stairs and opened the door of Mina's tiny apartment. Her exhaustion always seemed to lift for a moment when her four daughters rushed to meet her at the end of the day.

But this evening, when Irina, Lilya and Galina walked quietly over to their mother, their faces scared and downcast, Alla's exhaustion quickly turned to fear. *Where was Luba, the youngest?* Alla often arrived home to find Mina half-drunk, but tonight, the older woman was outraged. "You cannot look after your children," Mina shrieked at Alla, ". . . and, you have no husband."

"Where is Luba?" Alla screamed. Flushed and unsteady, Mina lunged at Alla. "The neighbor banged on the door this afternoon," Mina slurred as she began acting out the scene. "The woman who lives with you has far too many children," she said. "How can she possibly care for them? Give me the youngest one." Mina's eyes were ablaze as she mimicked her neighbor.

"What have you done with my daughter?" Alla shrieked. "Tell me!"

"The little one is gone . . ." Mina taunted. "She's with the neighbor . . . probably at the train station by now . . . you should thank me . . ."

Rage coursed through Alla's body. Determined to silence the older woman once and for all, Alla pushed her daughters aside. Grabbing a pillow from a nearby chair, she lunged towards the drunken woman and shoved the pillow hard against Mina's face.

"Take your children and get out of my home, you . . ." the old woman tried to scream, but the young mother wasn't listening.

The girls watched in horror. After a long and forceful struggle, Mina's drunken body eventually fell limp.

There was no time to lose. Grabbing her coat, Alla rushed for the door and began running towards the train station. *Please let me find her. Please let her be there.* She could hear a train approaching in the distance. She bounded up the platform stairs. By now, the train had stopped and the passengers were already boarding. Alla looked one way, and then the other. *There she was, right at the end of the platform!* "Luba! Luba!" her mother screamed. Running to the door of the train, Alla grabbed her daughter's arm and wrestled her out of the grip of the older woman.

Alla's entire body shook as she made her way back to the apartment. Holding tightly to her daughter's hand, she trudged up the stairs, opened the door . . . and gasped in disbelief. *Had she really suffocated Mina?* She'd seen people murdered in front of her, but she'd never thought *she* could kill another human being, certainly not with her bare hands.

Mina certainly appeared to be dead, *but what if she wasn't?* Suddenly panic-stricken, Alla shouted to Lilya, "Fetch the sharpest knife!" The girls' terrified screams were drowned out by a call to prayer from the nearby mosque as Alla and her daughter Lilya crouched down on the floor and began to sever the head from the old woman's body.

It was many hours before Alla and her daughters had disposed of the entire body, but by the end of the day, the deed was done, and Luba, who had been retrieved from the local railway station, was reunited with her mother and sisters. When the sun rose over Khujand the following morning, Alla woke up, said goodbye to her girls, and went to work.

As if nothing had happened, the little family simply continued to live in the elderly woman's house.

Eventually, some of the neighbors asked, "Where is Mina?"

"She's visiting relatives in Tashkent," Alla lied.

But before long, the neighbors became suspicious and called the police. After a short interrogation, Alla was sent to jail, Irina, who was eighteen at the time, was left to fend for herself, and the three younger children were sent to various orphanages, where they would live until they were sixteen years old. At that point, they too would be on their own, left to deal with the fallout of a traumatic and deeply confusing childhood.

◆ ◆ ◆

FIVE HOURS AWAY, THE CITY OF DUSHANBE, PREVIOUSLY KNOWN AS Stalinabad, had grown into a modern capital city by the time Galina was discharged from the orphanage where she had spent the past few years of her life. By now, Tajikistan was emerging towards independence, but key governmental positions were still held by ethnic Russians, and corruption was rife. Most importantly, Tajikistan remained the poorest republic within the Soviet Union.

Without any assistance, alone, and having lost all contact with her family, Alla's third daughter, Galina, had tried to make her own way in the city but was soon taken advantage of and found herself pregnant. A few months later, in a small village on the outskirts of Dushanbe, Galina met Rustam, an older Tajik man, and they began their life together.

Baby Angelica brought Rustam and Galina much joy, but when she was just learning to walk, she became very sick. "Take her straight to the hospital," Rustam instructed Galina. It was a difficult moment for them both. Rustam had struggled to find work and already they could barely afford their simple, daily food. How would they ever be able to pay for their daughter's medical bills?

But that night, when Rustam followed Galina to the hospital, he was greeted by terrible news. "She's gone!" shouted Galina in despair. "They gave her the wrong treatment." When the young parents heard that their daughter had been given the wrong injection instead of being treated for dehydration and jaundice, they were devastated. But when they returned that night to an empty house, their anger grew.

In blind fury, Rustam grabbed his axe. Racing back to the hospital, he seized the nurse who had treated Angelica and, dragging her along behind him by her hair, began smashing the walls and doors along the hospital corridor. Back at the house, Galina clutched her swollen belly. Like her husband, her mind was filled with torment. Visions of death haunted the couple day and night. A few months later, in the same hospital, my mother gave birth once again.

Добро пожаловать в мою историю—Welcome to my story.

CHAPTER ONE

WHEN I WAS BORN, PEOPLE SAID I HAD A CLOUD OF DEATH around me. I was a sickly baby, and from the moment I gave my first cry, my mother Galina lived in secret terror that she would lose me, just like she lost my sister two months earlier. In Tajikistan, it was common to make these sweeping statements, little suggestions that played on people's minds and troubled them in their sleep. But once the proclamation had been made, little more was said. *Why did bad things happen?* It was better not to talk about it. No one talked about the pain or the fear that tormented my parents day and night.

And although I never doubted I was loved, the 'cloud of death' was ever-present. The anger was present too. My father, Rustam, had a short temper, and my mother provoked him tirelessly. "When will you finish the house?" she kept asking. "Winter is coming, and there is no glass in the windows." My mother dreamed of the day their partially constructed house would be finished, but for my father, the topic only brought anger and frustration. While others in the village of Cheptura appeared to be leaving their poverty behind them, my parents seemed to sink lower and lower. Around and around they went, arguing about the house and about money.

Like a beast, the anger in our home grew stronger and more volatile with time until any little provocation could set it off on an angry rampage. I cowered in the corner, hoping the beast would tire or move to some far-off place, but the pain that consumed my parents was insatiable. Soon, their arguments became violent.

Two years after my sister Zarina was born, my mother decided she'd had enough. The day she ran away from my father, she took me with her, leaving my two-year-old sister behind. I was delighted when we finally went back to collect Zarina some months later, but the trauma of being abandoned had affected her deeply.

Having heard there was work in the neighboring country of Uzbekistan, my mother took me and my sister to live in Tashkent. *What a massive room,* I thought as I lay on my mattress that night. My mama had been offered a job as an assistant at a government-run kindergarten, and we were permitted to sleep in one of the classrooms. Each classroom had a section divided off for sleeping, a kitchenette, a play area . . . and a little garden! No wonder our bedroom felt so massive!

But my childlike awe was quickly shattered. Instead of finding freedom, my mother fell prey to terrible situations. Things started happening between my mother and men that left me terrified—even at four years old. Late one night, we were being driven home by a man who suddenly began shouting at my mother. "I will throw gasoline over you all and burn your children!" he threatened. The man wanted my mother to do something, but she refused. I can only imagine it was something that a child should not witness. I was scared to death.

Another night, a man came to the kindergarten searching for my mother. "Galina! Galina!" he shouted from outside. "Keep quiet!" Mama ordered us. "He will go if you keep quiet." For the first time in my life, I was paralyzed by fear.

By the time I was five or six years old, it wasn't just the men who made me afraid. It was also my mother. I knew my mother had a temper, and she had often punished my sister and me severely, but now her punishments became harsher. I had always been severely disciplined for wetting the bed at night. Now Mama began threatening me with her sewing needles. "If you wet your bed again, I will sew your vagina together," she shouted at me, holding a needle in front of my face. I remained terrified of wetting the bed right into my preteen years.

Mama came up with excruciating punishments. When I did something wrong, she would throw coarse salt down in the corner of the kitchen. "You kneel there until I say you can get up," she would yell at me. Sometimes I knelt for an hour or more, the sharp, gravelly grains cutting into my knees and making them bleed. I desperately wanted to move and ease the pain, but I was so afraid, I would stay there until I could barely get up again. I realize now that my mother's punishments weren't unusual in the culture I was brought up in, but still, they caused me great inner turmoil.

One morning, as I ran around inside—it was far too cold to go outside—I bumped into Mama as she was lifting a large pot of boiling water off the stovetop. She stumbled and the scalding water spilled all over me. My hands immediately began shaking with shock and pain. But instead of rushing me to the hospital, my mother began screaming at me. "Go outside and stand in the snow," she commanded. I went outside and stood there, nearly freezing in the cold, my hands blistering in pain. My mother stood out on the balcony above me. "Now walk back and forth in the snow," she yelled, ". . . and stay there." I was near fainting with the pain, but I kept walking back and forth because I was too terrified to do otherwise. That day, I learned that by disassociating from the pain, I could fulfil my mother's demands and, more importantly, survive. This ability was to become both a gift and a curse, as I would find out later in life.

THE DISSOLUTION OF THE SOVIET UNION WAS ON THE HORIZON, AND when I was six years old, a lot of Russian soldiers began leaving Tashkent. That's when my mother met a strong, handsome man named Nikolay, who had just left the army. They soon married, and Nikolay became our stepfather and the father of our half-brother, Yura. This marked a new beginning for our family. Hearing that my grandmother, Alla, had been released from prison, we decided it was time to leave Uzbekistan and return to Khujand, where most of my mother's sisters still lived. After seven years, her family was going to be reunited!

We moved into a government-owned, communal apartment building. Every floor housed thirty or more families. We shared a kitchen and a block of dismal toilets and showers with four other families. Each family was allocated only one room for both living and sleeping, no matter the number of children. The five of us were squeezed into a two-hundred-square-foot room.

Back in Khujand, Mama worked two jobs. I never knew what my stepfather did for work—he may have been a handyman—but he was always hardworking. I knew what my mother did because, to my delight, she sometimes took me with her to her evening job. She was beautiful, a talented traditional dancer, and she was often hired to dance at weddings. I would watch her approach each table, where she would perform with great passion, flicking her red skirt and swirling around the table. The men tucked money into spaces and pockets in her costume, which was part of the tradition and how a dancer was paid. There was plenty of alcohol at these weddings, and I watched Mama drink a lot.

After about a year, we moved into a rented studio apartment where we had our own kitchen and bathroom, but this was when things began to get worse. Mama and my stepfather Nikolay had been making good money in their jobs, but they had never saved any of it. When a recession hit, Nikolay began to steal. He soon took a bicycle and was caught, charged and imprisoned for a short time. This pattern of stealing and arrest repeated itself many times, and I hardly saw my stepdad except for about a month every so often when he was out of prison. Whenever he returned home, he was always kind to us. I have fond memories of Nikolay, and I still remember his warm smile.

However, on one arrival back home after yet another stint in jail, he and Mama had a furious argument. For the first time, Nikolay hit my mother, smashing her leg hard with a military baton. What happened next was horrifying and almost cost him his life. Seething with anger, Mama seized hold of the sharpest knife in the kitchen and grabbed my stepfather by his coat. We all watched in horror as she ran the knife into his chest a full nine or ten times. Then she thrust him out of the apartment and slammed the door shut. After a few minutes, Mama finally came to her senses and opened the door.

We all crowded around to see my stepfather lying in a pool of blood. The ambulance arrived after a long wait, and it was a miracle my stepdad didn't die. "I don't want to press charges," he whispered to the policeman who investigated. Maybe it was a miracle, but Mama wasn't taken to jail, nor us children to an orphanage. My stepfather survived, but he continued to be in and out of prison for the rest of my childhood. Deep inside, I longed for him to be my true papa, our protector, but I began to lose all hope that he would come back and make everything alright.

CHAPTER TWO

NIKOLAY NEVER DID MAKE EVERYTHING ALRIGHT. CIVIL WAR WAS brewing, and the recession bit sharply after the complete dissolution of the Soviet Union. The pro-communist groups fought to retain power in the face of an opposing alliance of Islamic forces. Both Russian communist and Islamic militias were burning their way through the rural farmlands, looting and destroying, trying to gain control. Many ordinary Tajiks who couldn't escape to their relatives in other nearby countries went to live in the overcrowded cities. Public services like schools and hospitals were in a run-down state, and business was nearly non-existent. Electricity and water supplies were often cut off, making the already cold Tajik winters longer and darker. There was a constant feeling of unease as armed men openly walked the streets. Murder, robbery, kidnapping of children and trafficking of young women became widespread. Much of the population survived on rationed food and subsistence handouts from international aid organizations. Around one-fifth of the population was displaced. People were sinking into deep poverty, and this included our family.

Mama lost both her jobs while my stepfather was still in prison. Alla, my grandmother who had often looked after us children, died, and Mama was left with three young children, no job and no social welfare. Every item was rationed at the local store, and Mama and I often worked at the food court, washing dishes in exchange for watery soup at the end of the day. I was now eight years old, and she had given me the job of keeping a place in the bread line for much of the night so I could be sure of receiving our daily ration when it was delivered.

As I stood outside the gated local store, the bread truck finally approached. It was five o'clock in the morning, and if I peered around the people in front of me I could see the truck turning the corner into the street. The previously ordered line became a jostling wave, with people jumping up from their sleeping places, desperate for bread. I unwrapped myself from my blanket so that I, too, would be ready. The hungry mob pushed and trampled one another to get to the truck. It was no place for a child, and I found myself fighting to stay upright. I felt like I couldn't find enough air to breathe. Someone reached down and helped me stand, but the hunger-driven surge was scary. I still had to make my way to the store gate to get our bread. I pushed through the crush of bodies, and somehow I managed to reach out and receive our meagre daily ration. The loaf was so soft and fluffy, that if I accidentally squeezed it with both hands it would turn into a small ball of dough before I reached home.

Our family was starving. Our studio apartment was falling into disrepair, the curtains were moldy and ripped, and we had no table. The toilet wouldn't flush anymore, and even as children, we thought this was disgusting. Mama sold everything she could to keep us fed. Soon, the only furnishings we had left were the old Tajik *kurpacha*,[1] some blankets, and a couple of metal chairs. Lying down on my cotton mattress one evening, I looked at the apartment walls to see hundreds of baby cockroaches darting from one hiding place to another. They were breeding persistently—just like the lice in our hair. Mama didn't have the emotional or physical energy to deal with three heads full of lice, so the next morning she simply shaved off all our hair. For a long time afterwards, I was taunted by other children shouting "Baldy" whenever I went out on the street to walk to school.

Zarina was seven and I was just turning nine, but already we had jobs selling newspapers door-to-door. Being used to making many of our own decisions, even at this age, we knew that this type of employment was a dangerous job for children. Nasty things had happened to some of the children in our neighborhood, and we knew about the dangers,

---

1 Cotton-filled mattresses

so we took precautions. I gave Zarina the rundown: "Never stand too close to the door in case we need to escape." Some children had been dragged into a house or had men unexpectedly expose themselves to them. "We always need to have a route to escape," I continued. "Whenever we go to a door, always look around and know which direction you will run if you have to." I taught my sister all my little tricks for staying safe, and we always went two-by-two. We also never went out selling door-to-door at night.

Whenever there was an electricity cut in the winter, our concrete building froze, leaving us with no way to heat our apartments or cook our food. We were constantly shivering and often sick, and we missed countless days of school. Everyone was struggling in our town, but we were one of the poorest families.

My only shoes had come apart at the soles, and I thought to myself, *If only I could mend them.* Mama couldn't do the task because she was out again. *I need a needle.* I hunted through my mother's box of mending things until I found a J-hook needle. *That will do.* It was difficult pushing the needle through the upper part of the shoe and then down into the sole. *Once more,* I told myself, *then it'll be finished.* I tugged the needle through the thick sole and pulled a bit too hard. My arm jerked up suddenly and the needle pierced my lower lip—it went right through! I could see the thread hanging from my lip with my shoe still attached to the other end. Mama wasn't there to help, and my little sister and brother thought I looked so funny—but I had to figure out how to free myself. Zarina brought me our only pair of scissors, and I carefully cut the sewing thread off the needle and then pulled the thread back through my lip, freeing my mouth from the shoe. *It was worth it for warm feet,* I decided.

Not only did we struggle for food and electricity, but also our water was limited. Thankfully, winter was passing, and the sun was beginning to shine on the snowy mountaintops that surrounded the city. We lived at the top of a hill, and Zarina and I would run laughingly down through the streets, a red bucket clutched in each hand. We knew we could find a tap in one of the government buildings, and we filled our four buckets, then carried them slowly and carefully back up the hill.

Summers were better than winters. We could forage for food, and the wonder of the summer warmth brought the trees to fruit. The three of us children were often out foraging—well, it was technically stealing—fruit from neighbors' gardens, the public parks, and any tree that had branches overhanging the street. Apples, pears, apricots—we threw them all into our bags, and some went straight into our mouths. One day, we arrived at one of the big apricot trees in the park, ready to fill our bags and bellies. Up we went, scrambling high into the laden branches, but moments later, a security guard arrived and stationed himself under our tree, enjoying the shade while he watched the park. We perched awkwardly in silence for a whole hour, hardly daring to shift our weight and get more comfortable, knowing what would happen if we were caught stealing. At last, the guard wandered off and the coast was clear. We jumped down from the tree and raced up the hill, proud to bring our fruit haul home. Even today, whenever I see a fruit-bearing tree sitting out on a public street, I stop and harvest a few. My childhood taught me to love even the sour green fruits. These were the happy moments I cherished, but underneath the lighthearted adventures there was always the hopeless despair of unending poverty—a relentless burden that weighed on us most of our days.

CHAPTER THREE

IT WAS SOON AFTER MAMA LOST BOTH HER JOBS THAT SHE STARTED to leave us alone at night. I was about ten years old when this started, and I remember sitting on the first-floor balcony of our studio apartment, calling for her in the night, hoping that somehow she would hear me. I was scared to stay at home by myself and to be responsible for looking after my siblings. The immense pressure on me—when I was a mere child myself—was overwhelming. But I sat on watch, my legs stretched out across the floor with a pillow on my feet. I had put Yura on the pillow and rocked him to sleep with my legs. When he cried, I pacified him with honey. No one had told me I shouldn't give honey to a young child, and no one told me that life would soon become much more difficult for us all.

◆ ◆ ◆

THE SMALL, OUTER BALCONY OF OUR FIRST-FLOOR APARTMENT LOOKED out onto the street. It was enclosed with a battered metal frame to protect the apartment from intruders, and a shabby curtain draped over the old frame gave us some privacy. Broken toys and unused items lay scattered across the cracked tile floor. Playing on our balcony one day, my little brother, my sister and I were not alone. Our mother had closed the balcony doors, but two fat-bellied men sat outside with us, seated on metal chairs. They had paid their money and were now waiting their turn to have sex with my mother or her friend Lala on our family's thin, cotton *kurpacha*. These mattresses, set out on the floor in the living room and kitchen, were the same mattresses we slept on.

Most afternoons, we played outside on the balcony or down in the street while our mother and Lala worked. At first, I had no comprehension of what was going on. As children, we did not grasp the full deprivation and despair that surrounded us; this was simply how we lived.

Too often, when my siblings and I were home alone and trying to sleep, men would come knocking on our door and asking for our mother. Late one night, we were all in bed and Mama, as usual, was out. There was a loud knock on the apartment door, and several male voices started calling for our mother. I went up to the locked door reluctantly. "My mother isn't home."

My answer was not enough for the men who started to yell and kick at the door. I could tell they were drunk, and I recognized one of the men's voices; he had been at our apartment before. The yelling and kicking intensified, waking up Zarina and Yura who began to cry. I knew that our door would not hold for much longer, and I was terrified. For some reason, I told my brother and sister, "Get down on your knees and pray!" We did not have much understanding of what that meant, but amid the terrifying shouts and poundings at the door, we asked God for help. Suddenly, the yelling and kicking stopped, and the men left—just like that.

MORE AND MORE MEN STARTED VISITING OUR APARTMENT, AND SOON all our neighbors and friends knew what was happening. One day, as Mama and I walked along the street, I overheard a man offering her a sheep in exchange for me. I heard the words, but I had no idea what they meant. Still, I felt a rush of shame, and I just wanted to disappear. This was the first time a man had focused on me, a child.

Our little apartment had turned into a brothel, and men would come and visit all day and late into the night. Sometimes Mama would have Lala or some of her other girlfriends stay in our apartment to help with 'business'. I liked Lala; she was a kind, gentle woman, but she often came to our place with bruises on her face, and this upset me.

"Have you got any children, Lala?" I asked her one day.

"No children." She shook her head "I used to live in Russia, but I fell in love with a man from Tajikistan. He promised to marry me, so I came here with him. But he beat me and left me with no money and no passport."

"Why don't you ask your family to help you so you can go back home?"

"I have done too much that is wrong," Lala replied softly. Her life seemed so sad. I knew there was much more to her story, but she wouldn't share it with me.

Our house was filled with alcohol, arguing, and, at times, fighting, especially when the men came. Mama began drinking heavily, and she would often take her anger, fear, and frustration out on us. The beatings became frequent and brutal—my brother, sister and I still have the scars to remind us. I was the eldest and received the most beatings, but the emotional abuse and neglect we all suffered were even more damaging.

As I grew into early adolescence, Mama became increasingly angry with me. I learned to be invisible around her, as the mere fact of my being in the room seemed to create trouble. Most days, Mama would work well into the night. During the day she would sleep, leaving us to feed ourselves and get to school. When she wasn't in the house, I would often transfer her anger towards me onto my sister Zarina. I was slowly becoming more violent, and I began to fight on the streets and at school. Sometimes I lost a fight and was beaten badly, but I didn't know how else to deal with what was going on in my home life. I was trying to hide my fear and hurt behind a facade of toughness. Already we had been labelled in the neighborhood as the children of a prostitute.

Nearly every evening, I stayed outside as long as possible to avoid the unpredictable horrors awaiting me at home. One night, I came home late and walked into absolute chaos. My younger sister and brother were asleep on the floor. But right beside them was my mother, drunk and dazed, while on top of her was our neighbor. Two more men hovered in the kitchen. I screamed at Mama to stop, but she swore at me nastily and told me to go away.

I stayed out all night, alone and shaking, afraid to go back inside. Finally, I crept up onto the roof of our apartment complex and locked the hatch of the roof's stairwell behind me. I found some old cardboard to sleep on and laid it out on the concrete floor. I covered myself with a pile of torn clothing and rags tossed in a corner and did my best to settle down. In the middle of the night, I heard the sound of someone trying to open the hatch. I was terrified that whoever it was would burst through and find me, but somehow, the lock held. I have no idea if my brother and sister slept through the depravities that took place in our home that night. Thinking about it still breaks my heart.

CHAPTER FOUR

NEXT DOOR TO US LIVED MY FRIEND ALLIE WHO WAS THE SAME age as me, and her little brother. Like us, they were the children of a single mother, but they seemed much better off. Their apartment was modest but clean, and they had more food available. Whenever I went to visit, Allie or her mama would always feed me, and I looked forward to the bit of extra sustenance for a stomach that seemed to be always hungry.

One day, I watched with eager anticipation as the pasta Allie was boiling bubbled away in the pot. When it was nearly done, Allie strained out all the water and poured a little oil into the pan. Frying the pasta added extra flavor, and when we sat down to eat, my mouth was watering. We ate with gusto, but Allie managed to eat and talk at the same time. "Let's go to Istikol tomorrow and visit my grandmother," she suggested suddenly. "We can pay for your bus fare." The two of us loved adventures, and I was pleased to be included in one that meant a journey.

We set off enthusiastically the next day with Allie's younger brother in tow, undaunted by the forty-two-kilometer bus ride. Chattering with excitement, we hailed the bus, then watched as it drove on by. Bus drivers sometimes didn't stop for children, believing they wouldn't be guaranteed payment. Undeterred, we decided to walk the whole way to Allie's grandmother's house. The trek took us all day, and the long journey became more and more difficult. We had no food or water, and Allie's six-year-old brother complained the whole way. In the end, we took turns carrying him.

The arduous trip was worth it—I loved being with Allie's grandmother. Like many of the houses in Istikol, hers was the German-style of architecture. Set in lovely tree-lined streets, the Germans had built these houses for the families who worked the nearby mines in the late 1800s. After the mining industry shut down in the early 1900s, the German workers returned home, leaving the town quiet and the houses and mines abandoned.

Allie's grandmother was exceptionally calm and kind . . . and she had plenty of food! We knew we'd be staying the night with her due to our late arrival, so we spent the rest of that hot summer day exploring the mines and swimming in the lakes that had been created by the unfilled pits. As an adult, I learned that these lakes had been formed by water collecting in abandoned uranium mines. The mines have been closed now for many years due to being unsafe and potentially toxic—yet we swam in those lakes as children!

A few weeks after our visit, Allie's grandmother sent her a beautiful book for her birthday, filled with illustrations. I was immediately drawn to this wondrous item, and I picked up the book with reverence, opening it to find a picture of a man surrounded by a crowd of children. The children were clustered all around him, and some were even climbing onto his knees. I stared at the image. It seemed to be . . . *alive!* The colors gleamed on the page, and there was so much life in that picture, it made me feel a sudden hope. At that moment, I felt as though a laughing, bubbling cascade of water was rushing down all over me, bathing me in joy.

Allie didn't seem to care for the book at all, so I offered her some money for it and took it home triumphantly. The book turned out to be a children's Bible. It was the first time I had seen a Bible, and while I didn't know anything about Jesus, that picture of him surrounded by laughing children planted a tiny seed of hope deep within my heart.

Tajikistan was a communist country, hostile to the idea of God, but it also had an ever-increasing Muslim population. My mother practiced a mix of superstition and pagan rituals. When Yura was sick, she took him to a hypnotherapist, and she knew a woman, a *folbin* or a witch doctor, who performed rituals such as killing a rooster and applying the blood to a sick person's body in various ways. Mama was interested in

Tarot cards and often did amateur readings for others—fortune telling was very much a part of our everyday culture.

On the other hand, my father and his family were all practising Muslims. In a simplistic and childlike way, I knew there was a God and that he would not punish me—that he would help me, somehow. Playing in the hills with my friends, whenever we would lie down to watch the clouds scudding across the sky, my thoughts would be drawn heavenward. *This is where God lives,* I would think to myself. *This must be his home.*

CHAPTER FIVE

I CAN BARELY COMPREHEND THE INDIFFERENCE OUR MOTHER HAD towards us, but as a child, I too learned to detach from my reality to survive. I became an angry girl, and I had plenty of reasons for being so. Violence was a regular part of my life and I was physically abused by my mother, often brutally. Mama was unpredictable and strong, and when she was angry she would lash out, either physically or with vicious verbal abuse. If I had upset her in the morning, she would scream death wishes at me as I left the house, shouting things like, "May a car hit you on your way to school." She called me hideous names, names too vile to repeat. Her vitriol hung over me like a heavy cloud.

I dreamed of a home where no one yelled at me or beat me up. *Can't I be a normal kid, just playing and enjoying life?* Instead, I lived on constant alert, with nobody to turn to for safety, and nobody to talk to about the abuse. Discussing our pain was not something anyone in our community would do, and besides, most of my friends were also experiencing abuse in some form.

In my teens, my anger spilled over into beating up my little sister when Mama wasn't around. The deep rage churning inside me led me to give my younger brother two serious beatings as well. I argued with my friends, and once, in a fit of wild anger, I yelled terrible insults at my friend Allie—horrible words that Mama had used on me. Allie's mother soon learned about this, and she asked me to come to her apartment for a chat. I was terrified, as she was a big, strong woman—I thought she was going to give me a good hiding! Instead, she had a quiet and mature conversation with me. "Marina, if you are upset, you can express your feelings using less violent language." She gave me what I thought were some silly examples, but I never forgot her kindness towards me, despite my behaviour—and I never insulted Allie again.

I often got into fights on the streets, trying to protect my siblings by defending them against bigger, stronger kids. One day after school, I heard a cry from out on the street and recognized my brother Yura's voice. I looked out the window to see him lying on the ground. A much older boy had knocked him down, and a mob of boys stood around him threateningly. Without any thought, I raced down the stairs of our apartment and out into the scene, diving straight into the mob with a yell of retribution. I punched that boy so hard that he avoided our family from then onwards. But as a budding young woman, I had other reasons to use anger as a form of protection for myself.

One summer evening, my cousin and I were out for a walk, when I saw a teenage boy biking towards us very fast. I had an uncomfortable feeling in my gut, but I didn't know why. As he rode by, he reached out and grabbed at my breast, then quickly sped away. I was so furious, I immediately turned and chased after him. I caught him, dragged him right off his bike, and beat him up badly. I even broke his bike. He escaped my wrath in the end, but I doubt he ever grabbed anyone like that again. Unfortunately, it was not the last time I would experience this sort of harassment from other youth.

Walking home from school one afternoon, my classmate and I became aware of a group of young guys approaching us from behind. As they sauntered past, one of them suddenly grabbed my breast. Anger rushed up within me, and I roared like an animal as I whipped around and hit him in the face with such strength he almost fell over. But he recovered quickly and attacked me again as I tried to fight him off. A car that had been driving past stopped beside us, and a man got out to help me. He was a bodybuilder and looked very strong, so the boys quickly turned their attention to him. He managed to resolve the situation by talking things through with them, using calm reasoning. To my surprise, they listened to him, and the one who had grabbed me even asked for my forgiveness. I gave him a curt nod—I just wanted to kill him.

Anger was all around me and within me. I couldn't escape its dark clutches, no matter which way I turned. By the time I was thirteen, I had attempted suicide twice. Both times I had cut my wrists, hoping to bleed to death, but both times I had stopped halfway through, sobbing, too scared to finish. I often imagined myself drowning and being carried away by the water, telling myself that Mama would be very sad to lose me. I just wanted to be loved and to belong. I know now that my mother did love me—in her own way—but she had no ability to express this love in the ways I so desperately needed.

CHAPTER SIX

CHILDREN WHO SHARE A SIMILAR LIFE STORY TO MINE OFTEN DON'T make it. Substance abuse, sex slavery and suicide can swallow them whole, robbing these precious lives of their true destiny and leaving only a glimpse of the people they once were. Only a few of my childhood friends made it into their early twenties.

Shahi was my age, about five years younger than her brother, Fahi. Despite both parents being mute, Shahi and Fahi could hear and speak perfectly. Their mother had abandoned them when they were little, and their father raised them. When I was twelve or thirteen, the three of us used to hang out a lot—until Fahi regularly began to ask me to go into his room with him, alone. I avoided him from then on. Later, I learned that Fahi would beat and rape his younger sister several times a week. Shahi became a prostitute and eventually died of AIDS.

Another close friend, Meri, was two years younger than me and lived in the same apartment block. Raised by a hard-working single mother, she and her brother were much better off than we were, and I never heard their mother abusing them. Despite this, Meri ended up a prostitute, just like Shahi. I could never understand why—it seemed as though she had more of a chance than any of us at making something of her life.

Another friend who lived on the fifth floor of our apartment complex was sexually abused by her father. When she told her mother about the abuse, her mother did nothing because she didn't want to lose her husband.

And Allie, who let me buy her children's Bible and whose mother and grandmother were so kind to me, eventually became a prostitute as well.

◆ ◆ ◆

WHEN I WAS AROUND THIRTEEN, I CONSIDERED YULIYA MY BEST FRIEND. In many ways, she was like me. Her mother used to beat her up, and Yuliya was constantly running away from home. The two of us often sought out abandoned apartments where we would sleep for a few days, away from our mothers' beatings. Three years older than me, Yuliya was sixteen and already drinking alcohol, smoking and sleeping around with men. I joined her in the smoking and drinking, but I wasn't interested in letting any man near me. To tell the truth, I wasn't really interested in smoking or drinking either—but it was what all my friends did. But often, when I was at parties, I would discreetly pour my vodka on the ground to get rid of it.

One day, Yuliya invited me to have dinner with her at her boyfriend's apartment. He picked us up in his car, and I realized, *He's twice her age at least.* We arrived at his apartment to find several other men there too, and I began to feel nervous. But I comforted myself with the thought, *Yuliya would never do anything that could harm me.* At the end of the evening, Yuliya decided to stay the night with her boyfriend. I slept on the floor in the living room with his male friends, but no one touched me. I was only thirteen—perhaps I looked too young, perhaps they weren't men who would force themselves on a child, or perhaps I was somehow being looked after. Whatever the case, they left me alone that night.

Sometime later, Yuliya invited me to go with her to a sauna. I had never been to a sauna, and I liked the idea of trying something new. I didn't realize Yuliya's boyfriend would be there too. The two of them slipped out into a separate sauna, but I could still hear everything they were getting up to. When her boyfriend casually walked into my sauna room, naked, and laughingly asked if I might join them, Yuliya called out, "Leave her alone, she's too young." Despite these awkward events, Yuliya and I remained friends. I think because, somehow, we were bound by our brokenness.

◆ ◆ ◆

MOST OF MY CHILDHOOD FRIENDS AND CLASSMATES EXPERIENCED ABUSE and ended up in very bad places. Yuliya herself was trafficked to Israel. Later, I found out she had escaped and returned home, but she suffered badly from the damage done to her. She became a drug addict, and later she had two children whom she gave up for adoption. She died of an overdose, still only in her early twenties.

So many abused children had nobody to turn to for help and suffered in silence. I remember them still, and I always will. I have often blamed myself for not being there for my younger brother and sister. I should have taken them with me when I ran away from home for good, later that year. Eventually, they learned to run away too, and my little sister, Zarina, became especially good at it. However, the problems didn't go away once we left home—we had nowhere to run to except the streets. We had no safe place to live, and no relatives willing to care for us. We were completely and utterly alone.

CHAPTER SEVEN

I REMEMBER ONE PARTICULAR WINTER'S NIGHT AS THOUGH IT WERE yesterday. I was thirteen, drinking and celebrating New Year's Eve. A group of friends and I were going from party to party, and as we laughingly made our way from one venue to the next, I looked up at the night sky and thought, *There must be more to life than this. In fact, I know there is—but I have no idea how to get there.* That was the moment I decided to end my life once and for all. I knew that this time I would not 'try' but succeed. My desperate longing for a different kind of life was being painfully destroyed by an unbearable lack of hope. I truly believed that anything different from the life we currently lived was impossible.

Most of my friends were from dysfunctional families like mine and were also involved in a lifestyle of growing self-destruction. Many of them had been raped by the age of twelve or thirteen, and I knew it was only a matter of time before something terrible like that happened to me.

Spring came around, and I turned fourteen without any anticipation whatsoever for the future. I decided to write Mama a letter explaining why I was taking my own life. I hid the letter at home before going to school, expecting that she would find it later on, as I wanted to see my friends for the last time. I had heard of a neighbor poisoning her husband by putting mercury in his vodka, so I planned to do that to myself. Before leaving home, I broke our two thermometers and collected the mercury in a matchbox. Now I was ready for what I was going to do after school.

After a day of pretending all was normal, I was just leaving the school building when someone unexpectedly stopped to speak to me. A mere acquaintance and, like me, a young girl living a self-destructive life, she was not someone I'd have thought to look to for hope. "I'm on my way to a church service in the community centre," she said quietly.

"Do you want to come with me?" I had no idea what church was, other than the occasional glimpse I'd seen on television—sad-looking women in headscarves lighting candles at the altar in a Russian Orthodox church. I didn't want to go, but I found myself answering, "Yes!" Somehow, I was drawn to go with her then and there.

The community centre was big and bright. Young people like me were streaming into the auditorium in groups, and I realized this church was run by Korean missionaries. I sat down slowly, wary of the others packed around me. Then the people on the stage began to sing, and what I experienced at that moment was like nothing I had ever felt before. A powerful, invisible, loving presence approached me. It was beside me and all around me, embracing me. And with this presence came a deep understanding that I belonged, that I was loved and wanted. In a single breath, this profound knowing undid years of rejection, at the same time mending my shattered heart and filling me with a sense of love so pure, I sat with my face in my hands and wept and wept.

I had never cried like that before. Crying was not something I did much—my mama was never comfortable with my emotions, and it was not safe to express feelings of sadness, anger, or pain. So I had bottled them all up inside me. Now, for the first time in my life, I felt safe to express them. My emotions poured out in tears, streaming freely from my heart as I encountered my Maker—the one I had longed for all these years but had never realized I could meet. All thoughts of suicide completely left my mind.

A few months later, as I began to understand more of the grace I had encountered, I wrote down some of my thoughts as I read in the Bible from Lamentations chapter three: "You came near when I called you, and you said, 'Do not fear.' You, Lord, took up my case; you redeemed my life" (v. 58).

I didn't fully understand it back then, but this is exactly what happened when I stepped into that church and was met by God himself.

I wrote:

My dear Lord Jesus, I am so grateful for what you have done for me at the cross. Thank you for your precious blood. Your blood has cleansed me from all my sins and you're filling me now with life. You delivered me through your sacrifice because of your love for me. You washed me whiter than snow. My Jesus, my love.

Ever since that day, and even now when I pause to soak in his presence, I still cry. Not because I am sad or in pain, but because I love him so much. I feel his love and kindness so tangibly. I feel safe with my Maker. He holds my emotions, no matter how big they are. He holds them with so much gentleness and love that the heavy scales—built up from years of neglect, abuse and trauma—fall off, just from my being with him.

CHAPTER EIGHT

U P UNTIL THE DAY OF MY ENCOUNTER WITH GOD'S PRESENCE, I had no idea about the Creator of all things. I had heard about Jesus and had even read the children's Bible I bought from my friend Allie when I was eleven, but I had no idea at all about the Trinity—that is, God the Father, God the Son, and God the Holy Spirit, and how they are one. After a while, I learnt to embrace the reality that I have always been part of this unity in all its glorious fullness. I am not—never have been and never will be—separated from the love of my Maker.

Experiencing God's presence brought me to understand that the Creator of all things is my parent—both my mama and my papa. Somehow, my childhood had not made me embittered and resentful, or even fearful, of God. If anything, the embrace of his love was starting to melt away the hate I had begun to cultivate against humanity.

Almost as if someone had flicked on a switch, things became clear and made more sense to me. My Maker gently taught me core values; how to keep my word and to always tell the truth. Many of my self-destructive behaviours—smoking, getting drunk, and thinking about trying to kill myself—dropped away, but I still held a lot of anger inside.

Even though I was now a believer in God, I was in the very early stages of understanding. I felt refreshed and filled with the wonder of my experience and in awe of the One who is so much bigger and greater than me. But on the street and in my home, there were still so many struggles.

In frustration and anger, I ran away from home again during the summer school holidays. My best friend Yuliya had had a big fight with her mama, and she had left home too. She found an abandoned apartment on the fifth floor of an old building, and so we decided to live there together.

The tiny balcony of our apartment overlooked a shaded inner courtyard. Although the building had once been painted a pale pink, mold and dirt concealed almost every trace of color. I looked out into the courtyard below, noting countless clotheslines strung from balcony to balcony, weighed down with grey-looking towels, sodden bedding, and clothing drying slowly in the dreary sunlight.

A next-door neighbor was pegging washing on her line, and she didn't see me surreptitiously watching her. I was waiting to grab the cotton bag of old bread crusts that she hung on her line nearly every day to dry them out. By leaning over the balcony as far as I could possibly stretch, I could just reach out and grab the bag.

Even though the bread was moldy, I ate a few crusts quickly before pegging the bag back onto the line, trusting the neighbor wouldn't notice. At home when we were hungry, Mama had always given us the moldy bread crusts. "It's just penicillin," she'd say.

I urgently needed a job, and Yuliya had an idea. "Come and meet Nasim," she suggested. "I've heard that he can get anyone a job. He's a family friend, and I'm sure he could find you something that would pay well for a day or two if you're interested."

Of course I was interested—I needed the money.

I agreed to meet Nasim at Yuliya's mother's apartment while her mother was present. Nasim did have a job for me—a package needed urgent delivery by hand to Moscow. Apparently, it contained rare and expensive car parts that couldn't be sent through the mail system.

"I can put you on tomorrow night's train to Moscow," he told me. "Once you arrive at the station, someone will meet you to collect the package. Then he'll put you on the next train back home." Nasim promised that, on my return, he would pay me a very generous sum for acting as his courier.

Feeling a bit cautious and uncertain, I nevertheless agreed to make the delivery. *This man is a friend of Yuliya's family,* I reasoned. *Surely he's reliable. Besides, this is good money for such an easy task. I'll only be away for an overnight train trip.*

Since I had run away from home, I didn't tell my mother about the trip or ask her for permission to go to Moscow. That evening, Nasim took me to the local market to buy some smart clothes for the journey. I was doing business, he said, and I would need to look good. As we wandered in and out of the market stands, he chatted to me about his wife and family. The clothes he bought for me were better than any clothes I had ever owned, but to my mind, they didn't seem very suitable for a fourteen-year-old girl living in a Muslim country.

Nasim took me back to his apartment for a meal before the train left later that night. I had expected his family to be there, but to my surprise, I soon realized we were alone. Then Nasim attempted to abuse me sexually. I'd never experienced anything like that before, even though I had seen plenty of men abusing my mother. I froze. I could not scream or even fight.

Looking back, I believe what happened next was another example of God's intervention—I cannot explain it any other way. Nasim simply couldn't get an erection. He tried touching me, but nothing happened. He went out of the room, and I ran to the toilet, locking myself inside. He soon found me and forced the door open, but just then I heard voices outside the apartment and I ran to the balcony to shout for help. But I didn't dare call out when I saw the voices belonged to a group of three men down on the ground floor. For some reason, Nasim decided to leave me alone. He went into the other room to sleep, but I couldn't sleep at all. In the early hours of the morning, he shouted at me in frustration, "Go! Get out of here!"

There had been no sign of a package all night, and now I realized. *The package I was to deliver to Moscow was **me**! I had blindly walked into a trap, and Nasim had been assigned to break me.*

I was enraged and ready to thrash Yuliya. I had trusted her—she was my best friend! By the time I made it back to our apartment, I found out she had spread rumors to our school friends, telling everyone I had sold myself to a man and was now a prostitute. Everyone was buzzing with the news that I now slept around.

Why did she do that? She had set me up. *And she was probably paid for her part in bringing me to Nasim,* I fumed.

Smarting from the betrayal, Yuliya and I went our separate ways. We never spoke again.

◆ ◆ ◆

IN THE CHURCH WHERE I'D HAD MY FIRST ENCOUNTER WITH GOD, I soon found a sense of belonging and made some good friends. The rest of my fourteenth year saw me spending less and less time at home. Even though my life outside home had greatly improved, it was still traumatic for me to be there. Christians were a minority in our city, but the political and economic instability following the collapse of the Soviet Union in our country worked in our favor. The government didn't pay much attention to churches and home groups, even though Christians were still being persecuted in some of the smaller villages. My new friends and I were the outcome of an ongoing revival that had been started by Korean missionaries who had come to live in our city.

Every day after school, for the rest of the year, I headed straight to church, home group or church-related volunteer work. The Korean church offered transportation to everything, which was a real blessing for me as I had no money for the bus.

As part of our church activities, my friends and I often volunteered at different places around the area. One such place was a private local orphanage started by Rune and Kari Borgso, two Christians from Norway. We went once a week to help them out, often working in the kitchen. To me, this orphanage was an amazing place. Rune and Kari gathered children who were living on the streets and brought them back to care for them. The orphanage provided a safe, clean, and nurturing environment. There was lots of food to eat, toys to play with, and—most importantly—kind caregivers. In comparison, the only other orphanage in the city was government-funded, and it was not one you would want to end up in. I remember Mama used to threaten to send me there when she was upset. There were certainly a few times during my growing-up years when I had actually hoped I *would* go there—I thought it couldn't possibly be any worse than my life at home.

As well as volunteering at the private orphanage, my friends and I helped a blind, elderly couple called Vitaliy and Oksana. We cleaned and cooked for them in their house, and we often sat down and had a meal with them. I thought Vitaliy and Oksana were so cool—they were very kind and treated us well, and we enjoyed a lot of great conversations. My heart began to feel lighter. These people were not trying to extort me or use me. They simply allowed me to use my gifts to serve them.

One evening, a friend from church organized a private dinner at Vitaliy and Oksana's place. This was separate from our usual volunteer work, as my friend wanted to introduce me to another Christian couple, Arthur and Larisa Musayelyan, who lived in the area. Arthur and Larisa were pastors of a small church nearby, and they had told my friend they wanted to meet me. After dinner, Arthur and Larisa asked if they could pray for me. I accepted, and as they prayed, their words seemed to come from the very heart of God. I wept as my heavenly Papa spoke words of comfort and healing to me through their prayers.

That night, I wrote in my journal:

> *"I love you so much, I won't be able to live without you, Jesus. You are everything to me. There was a time when I was absolutely nothing, I hated my life, I could not love, I was simply nobody in this world, I was unwanted. You changed everything. I am so glad to hear that you do not need anything from me—just my heart. Thank you that you exist and that you love me without any conditions. Thank you for your justice; you never judge, and you know what is happening in my heart.*

The one thing I desire most is to always be near you—always— and when I do not have the strength to hold onto you, please hold onto me and never let me go. You are the most precious one in my life. People who've had an encounter with you will never be able to live without you. I am one of them."

I didn't know that both Arthur and Larisa, as well as Rune and Kari from the orphanage, would later play significant roles in my life and my ongoing journey of healing.

CHAPTER NINE

SINCE MY PROFOUND ENCOUNTER WITH GOD, I WAS SLOWLY LEARNing how to deal with my anger. God's love was softening my heart, and it was just the beginning of a lifelong process which ultimately revealed that my anger was merely masking the fear, hurt, sadness and grief that I carried. At school, my classmates immediately noticed the difference in me. One of them told me that she now believed in God because she had seen what he was doing in my life. I think this gives an idea of the beautiful work that was going on in my heart. But while I was indeed becoming softer—I never hit my sister Zarina again—I still had a long way to go with managing and healing my anger.

Looking back, I know that if I had felt safe and accepted, and if I'd had a sense of belonging as a child, my anger could have been addressed a lot sooner. The day I encountered God's love was the same day my constant need to be prepared for the worst and to disassociate from trauma began to fade away.

The church activities I was involved in kept me busy from morning until late at night—and I loved it. Mama, however, did not like me being away so much; maybe because it meant I did less to help at home. One evening, she yelled an ultimatum: "You choose right now between church and home!"

I chose church, and at fourteen years old, I walked away from home for good. I had nothing with me and nowhere to go. That night, I slept on the roof of our apartment complex, and for the next few weeks, I stayed in an abandoned apartment or with different friends here and there for a night or two. It was the summer holidays, and I needed money. I found some small jobs waitressing and washing dishes, which earned just enough to cover the cost of food but nothing else.

These were tough and difficult times, yet I had Jesus, and I was growing more and more in love with him, which gave me strength to keep going. But having cycled through all my friends who could have me stay a few nights, I soon ran out of options. Then I remembered Vitaliy and Oksana, the blind, elderly couple who had been so kind to me when I was volunteering my time to assist them. I nervously approached them and asked, "May I come and stay with you for a few days?"

Their immediate answer was, "Yes."

I NOW HAD A MORE STABLE ROOF OVER MY HEAD, BUT IT TOOK ME A while to feel secure living in their home. On one of my first nights, I was horrified when I awoke to find I had wet the bed. I was terrified of what they would say, and I tried to hide the wet stain. As a child, I had been severely punished for wetting the bed, but the reaction from Vitaliy and Oksana was completely different to my childhood experience.

Arriving back later that day from my waitressing job, I saw my mattress hanging out in the sun. *Do I say anything? Should I say sorry?* Vitaliy and Oksana said nothing, and neither did I. They were very kind and never scolded me for anything. I would have loved to stay with them forever, but after a week they decided that they could not look after me and that the local orphanage, run by Norwegian missionaries, would be a better place for me. Sure enough, when we arrived at the Helping Hands Orphanage—a private establishment run by Rune and Kari—they were able to make room for me that same day.

I remember very little from my first week there, and I don't think I said much either. The orphanage administrator needed my birth certificate, so two of the workers drove me to my mother's apartment to collect it. I was reluctant to see Mama. "No, I don't want to go inside," I replied when they tried coaxing me.

I waited silently in the car while one of the volunteer workers went inside to ask for my birth certificate. Mama gave the official certificate to the worker without asking to see me or finding out if I was all right. I chose to believe that she intuitively knew I was in good hands and was simply letting me go.

I had been at the orphanage for about one week when a long weekend came around. Seeing I was the only child without a place to go for the holiday, Rune and Kari asked, "Would you like to stay with us for a couple of days?" Well, a couple of days turned into a couple of weeks and then a couple of months, and in the end, I never went back to live at the orphanage.

Rune and Kari became my first foster parents. They were in their early thirties and had two sons—a three-year-old and a baby. The eldest boy was an absolute delight and already spoke the basics of four different languages: Norwegian, English, Russian and Tajik. The baby was as sweet as a baby could possibly be, and I adored both children.

Soon after I had moved in with Rune and Kari, we all shifted into a different house in Khujand. Kari walked me up to view the second floor of their new home, but I had no idea what she wanted to show me. We climbed up the most beautiful, white spiral staircase that led into a small bedroom at the very top of the house. "This is your room, Marina," Kari told me gently.

At first, I was quiet. I couldn't understand what she was saying; I had never thought I would have my own room. Finally, I spoke. "Really?" Here I was, fifteen years old, and for the very first time in my life, I had my own bedroom.

The room was small and basic—just a metal-framed single bed and a chest of drawers—but to me it was a mansion. A single window looked down onto the little garden below, and I could hear birds twittering in the trees and pigeons cooing on the nearby rooftops.

This is my room! I thought with joy. I loved that room, and I loved dancing up the spiral staircase and into my own private sanctuary. There was one stair about halfway up that creaked in a friendly sort of way whenever I stepped on it. Those stairs characterized safety for me—no one could sneak up on me, because I could always hear my creaky stair whenever someone ascended.

Years before, I'd had a dream about a spiral staircase. It had been white and graceful, with a slim handrail that floated up along the stairs—just like this one that led to my new room. What a luxury! What an impossibility. Until this time, I had never had a moment to myself and had longed fruitlessly for my own little corner. At home, we had all slept in one room on the floor, on old, smelly mattresses.

Later, I learned that neglect, abuse, trauma, and living in constant survival mode can drastically diminish a child's creativity and critical thinking. It also affects their ability to problem solve, and, most importantly, to dream. Miraculously, despite my upbringing, I'd held onto one or two very special dreams. I don't know why I'd dreamt about this room and its spiral staircase in such detail, but here it was in Rune and Kari's home. As I soaked in the wonder of this miracle, I remembered again the dreams and hopes I'd harbored as a child—that someone would rescue us and make things alright. Now, that desperate longing to belong, to feel safe, and to have my basic needs met, was finally coming true.

As my heart grew ever softer, I decided I wanted to visit my father. This bothered my mother, who said she hated him and wanted none of us to have anything to do with him. But as I wasn't living with Mama anymore, I made my own choice to go and see him. The journey was a long and expensive one for a fifteen-year-old, but I had such a longing to know my father. I traveled 200 miles through the mountains from Khujand to Cheptura where my dad, Rustam, still lived in the same little house he'd once shared with Mama, Zarina and me. Now he had a new wife and four daughters.

When I arrived, I noticed the house was still just as Mama had described it—a construction site. There was hardly any furniture, and I was given the only bed they had. The house was infested with fleas, making it unbearable for me to sleep at night. I had no idea how they lay down to rest in such conditions. Even though my father was a very hard worker and was on a good wage as a welder, they still lived in poverty. His current wife was not good with money, and his daughters often stole from him. I only spent about a week in their home, and I was eager to leave after that. My father and I did not have many meaningful conversations, but I did find a chance to share my new faith with him. He cried when I left, and I could see how much he loved me—you just know these things.

◆ ◆ ◆

I HAD NO IDEA WHAT LIVING IN A NORMAL FAMILY WOULD BE LIKE, though I'd always longed for such an experience. Life with my new foster parents was the complete opposite of the life I'd had before I met them. In particular, this family practiced some lovely, life-giving traditions that were so beautiful to me. Every Saturday morning, Rune would make up a tray of drinks and snacks for the whole family, including me, to share. Other times I would join them in their bedroom with the children, as we all sat down with a hot drink and a biscuit, chatting contentedly. There were no outbursts of rage or sudden beatings, and slowly I began to settle into a different kind of 'normal' within a family.

Kari treated me like a daughter, without the added layer of cruelty I'd experienced from my own mother. When she asked me if I'd like her to pierce my ears, I said yes, and then cried like a baby during the whole process. After the holes in my ears had healed, she handed me a pair of her gold earrings to wear, but I lost one of them. I felt so scared. I expected Kari to be angry and to shout at me, but she merely smiled and said, "It's alright, Marina," even though the earrings were special to her.

Rune was just as kind as his wife. I avoided letting people see me smile, and I often hid my mouth with my hand when I smiled. I had a gap where a tooth hadn't grown properly, and I felt so self-conscious I'd often find myself pressing the gap with my tongue. Then my other teeth shifted towards the gap and became crooked as well. But Rune would encourage me to smile, saying, "You have such a beautiful smile, Marina. It makes other people happy when they see you smile."

I loved eating five or six apples a day, but Kari told me they were used to eating only one apple a day, as apples were so expensive back in Norway. This was hard for me to comprehend. Fruit—even unripe—was a key part of my diet, and eating just one apple a day seemed strange. I smile at that now. But I also remember a time when I would feel hungry but also feel too afraid to eat their food. Sometimes I would say, "I'm not hungry," when they asked me to eat with them, even if I was ravenous. I was afraid that if I ate too much, they would ask me to leave. My damaged heart was still in the process of being healed.

◆ ◆ ◆

I GRIEVE THE FACT THAT ZARINA, YURA AND I DID NOT HAVE A STRONG bond as children and that we had lived in survival mode most of the time. Witnessing what was happening at home and not being able to change anything was tough. I cared deeply about my siblings and felt protective of them both. Nevertheless, I had no choice but to watch helplessly as Zarina and Yuri were continually exposed to an environment that robbed them of their innocence and their precious time as children. Still, I did what I could, even after I left home for good. My greatest desire was to bring Zarina and Yura to the orphanage which Rune and Kari had started. At one point, after hearing that Zarina had run away from home yet again, Rune and Kari stepped in and brought her to live with us for a time.

Strangely, I reacted to Zarina being under the same roof as me by being awfully mean to her and controlling her every move. The truth is, I was afraid she would jeopardize my relationship with Rune and Kari, and then they would kick us both out. At times I was a terrible sister towards her, and I still regret these incidents deeply. Zarina was only thirteen at this point, and in the end, she left and ran back to our Mama.

Little did I realize that my time with Rune and Kari was also about to be cut short—not because of anything I could control, but because just three and a half months after my arrival, Tajikistan descended into full-blown civil war.

CHAPTER TEN

AS THE POLITICAL CLIMATE IN TAJIKISTAN BECAME INCREASINGLY volatile, Kari and Rune prayed, "Lord, show us what to do. The country is at war. Should we stay or should we go?" Leaving wasn't an easy option. *What would happen to the orphanage? And what about me?*

Kari and Rune held out as long as they could. But on October 14th, 1998, an extremist group, seeking to establish an Islamic caliphate in the region, carried out a well-coordinated attack on a military base in our city. Dozens were killed in the violence and chaos that ensued, but it was only the start. Later that day, a riot broke out in the city prison, and over a hundred prisoners, many of whom had been convicted of serious crimes and were linked to extremist militant groups, broke free. The government responded with a full-scale manhunt, but when soldiers filled the streets and bullets started landing in the grounds of the orphanage, Kari and Rune knew it was time to evacuate. "Let's move the children to another location where they can be cared for by the young people from the church," they decided.

A few nights later, Kari had a dream. God's word to them was clear: "You must flee. It is dangerous to stay. Get out!" Kari and Rune were used to God leading them like this. There was no doubt in their mind that the situation was urgent. I, on the other hand, couldn't understand what was happening when Kari and Rune locked the door to their lovely house, bundled us all into their car, and after some hours, arrived at an apartment belonging to one of their friends. It was a whole day before I realized that my new foster family, along with all the other foreign workers, were about to leave the country and that I would have to stay behind.

My heart ached as they held me close. "Marina, we can't take you with us. You're still only fifteen, which means you're legally underage to make this decision for yourself. But we can't choose for you either, as there isn't time to go through the adoption process."

But what will happen to me? I thought.

I didn't hear the core truth behind these sudden decisions: *Rune, Kari and the little ones must flee for their lives immediately.*

Instead, in my brokenness I heard, *We do not love you as much as we love our own children, and so we will not fight for you. Our own family is more important to us.*

I believed this lie and saw it as another rejection—further proof that I was not lovable. It haunted me for years, robbing me of joy and gratitude for what was right in front of me. I believed the falsehood so strongly that it was hard to see myself in a different light. Eventually, I began to recognize my pattern of self-sabotage and how unhealthy it was.

Despite my broken heart, there was something life-giving in Kari's words to me as she left—words I carried with me for years after our abrupt and forced separation. "Marina, the way God took care of you up until today, is the same way he will continue to take care of you," she told me in her soft, Norwegian accent. I truly believed her, and in the difficult times that followed, I clung to those words.

I know God's care remained with me because, just a few days after Rune and Kari left, Arthur and Larisa contacted me through Helping Hands. I had met them earlier that year in the home of Vitaliy and Oksana.

"Marina, would you like to come and live with us?" Larisa asked. "You know, God told us to take you in the first time we met you, but Rune and Kari beat us to it!" she laughed. I was overjoyed when I heard that.

Arthur and Larisa were pastors of a small church, but they had no salary or mission supporters—they relied entirely on God's provision for their young family of two children, and now me. They taught me how to trust God for every need, and they modelled their love for God and for other people right in front of me. Prayer and Bible reading were part of their daily routine, but they never pushed it on me. I loved watching and hearing Larisa whenever she was talking to God and worshipping—there was so much love, passion, and authenticity in her adoration of Jesus.

Those were beautiful years, but at the same time, for me, they were also very tough.

Even though God was healing me, I was still in so much pain that the only way I knew how to deal with it was to shut down. In those moments, I felt trapped in a cloud of darkness and could see no hope at all. I spoke less and less, often not talking at all, and my face became a blank façade, not displaying any emotion.

These 'shutdowns' were heavy with grief and the struggle to express my emotions. *If only someone would speak gently to me and reassure me. "It's okay, we understand. We love you."* People said to me, "Marina, when you're happy, the whole room lights up. When you're not, everyone can feel it." But at the time, neither Arthur, Larisa, nor I knew how to speak about my 'shutdowns'. Still, they continued to love me in the best way they could.

◆ ◆ ◆

SLOWLY, LIFE BECAME MORE STABLE AND SECURE. I WAS STILL ATTENDING school, and I still visited Mama and my brother and sister as often as I could.

I loved Mama deeply, and my heart longed for a change in her circumstances. Perhaps, I thought, this could happen now—Mama was quite ill and getting worse. She had been diagnosed with cirrhosis of the liver caused by her excessive drinking.

"Get me another vodka, Marina," she called to me.

"Mama, how can you even think about drinking?!" I was stunned. It seemed so stupid that even with her diagnosis, she continued to drink.

"God," I prayed when I got back home to Larisa and Arthur's place, "Please heal Mama, please protect her, please provide for Yura and Zarina." Filled with determination, I declared, *Lord, I'm going to pray for them every day until a change happens.* I truly believed that my mama's story of healing would become a great testimony for the whole of Tajikistan.

Many friends supported me in fasting and praying for my family. Some even joined me in visiting my mother. I think their visits lifted her spirits, and she was glad I had good friends. She had always loved people, and she enjoyed seeing my world and my friends.

◆ ◆ ◆

ONE MORNING AS I WAS GETTING READY FOR SCHOOL, A PHONE CALL came in from Zarina.

"There's something wrong with Mama. She's really sick, she's scream-ing and shouting—listen!"

I could hear Mama in the background, screaming in fear. I immedi-ately rushed over to the apartment. There, I found Mama in an alcoholic delirium. She was crying and shouting, "I can see *'cherty'*!" She could see demons.

Oh God, I will not be afraid—but I was panicking inside—*how do I pray?* I began mustering all the confidence and authority in Jesus Christ that I could, begging God to replace the fear filling the atmosphere of the entire apartment.

When the ambulance arrived, I climbed inside with Mama. *She looks so frail and small,* I thought. I was still trembling inside with the tension and distress of what was happening.

She came to her senses for a moment and looked at me. "This is it, Marina. I'm dying."

"No, you are not, Mama." I tried my best to sound strong, and I kept praying as we sped to the hospital.

The nurses admitted my mother to the drug and alcohol rehabilita-tion clinic, and she was given a bed in an old ward that housed another woman. Cockroaches darted in and out of the dirty corners, their long, flat bodies and thread-like antennae a reminder of the infestation in Mama's apartment. *How can they even call this place a clinic?*

After school, I went back to visit her again. The ward she shared with the other woman stank, and it soon became obvious that Mama could not even take herself to the bathroom. There was only one nurse, slowly working her way through her duties for the day, and Mama hadn't even been attended to yet. She lay in her soiled nightdress on a wet and dirty bed. I felt angry, but also resentful that I would have to care for my mother simply because of the choices she had made. But I had no other options. The sense of responsibility for my family weighed heavily on my shoulders.

In Tajikistan, there is no free medical treatment. The clinic was short-staffed and underfunded, and in the end, my church raised money to pay for all of Mama's vitamins, pain relief and medications, as she underwent alcohol withdrawal. I decided to stay with Mama at the hospital. There, I slept as best I could on the spare *kurpacha* in her room. I stayed away from school for over a month, but no one followed up to check on my studies. It was not unusual for me and many of my friends to take extended time off school.

There was no portable toilet or bedpan in the clinic's ward, so I had to hold Mama up over a big, dirty, metal bucket—it didn't even have a wooden toilet seat attached. I attended to all of Mama's needs myself and was only ever assisted twice by a nurse. Mama's sheets needed washing daily, as she woke up every morning having wet the bed. Roaming the clinic, I found a large bucket in one of the toilets, and I used this to wash her sheets with cold water and a chunk of soap I had found in the bathroom. Someone had set up a clothesline in the dilapidated courtyard, and I hung the sheets to dry in the sunlight.

"Marina, how can I eat this mush when you push it in my face like this?" Mama hit me across the head. She was angry with me again, saying I was feeding her too fast.

Another daily trial involved trying to coax her to exercise. "You need to get up, Mama. You have to walk three times a day." It was terribly hard to help her because she kept rejecting my input.

One day, I'd had enough. As she lay in bed vomiting, I simply left her—I let her lie there and watched her impassively. *You don't like my care, so I'm not going to offer it anymore.* A nurse came in and asked what was happening, but I stayed where I was and didn't say anything. I was still very angry and resentful towards my mother. I could not understand why she abused us, her own children. I couldn't understand her choices to drink and prostitute herself.

On my sixteenth birthday, I was outside handwashing Mama's sheets in the big bucket when I saw Larisa walking along the street. I almost burst into tears. My heart was aching with hurt, anger, and sheer exhaustion.

"Marina, come here." Larisa enfolded me tightly in her arms as I brokenly told her how awful things were.

"Let me take over with your mama for today," she said gently. "Go home for the night, have a bath, have a good meal. Arthur is there and you can talk to him."

I went home, and the relief of a hot bath and a good night's sleep in the midst of such chaos was yet another wonderful gift that Arthur and Larisa gave me. Their kindness is something that will remain in my heart forever.

After a month at the clinic, Mama felt much better and returned home to her apartment. I was hopeful that this would mark a change for her, but she soon returned to her old lifestyle. There were no other alternatives she could see, and despite my prayers, she began drinking again.

◆ ◆ ◆

EVEN THOUGH THERE WAS NO CHANGE IN MY MOTHER'S LIFE, I FOUND myself greatly strengthened by my time with Arthur and Larisa. I benefited from the stability of the healthy, loving environment they provided during my teen years—it made all the difference to me. When I finished school at seventeen, Arthur and Larisa helped me to transition into a more independent life, setting me up in an apartment with a few friends.

I began studying choreography at a free, local college, but my main interest lay in the voluntary work I did with the youth mission segment of Helping Hands. This non-profit organization not only ran the orphanage, it also worked with youth in the city. I started out as a volunteer, but I was soon onboarded as a youth social worker. This became an incredibly rewarding time in which I gained many skills and made lasting friendships. Helping Hands took kids off the streets and gave them real opportunities for a positive life. We visited local schools and led various after-school activities, and we often took kids hiking in the mountains around Khujand. As a paid employee, I became the coordinator of these activities. With only a few volunteers to help me, I found myself trained 'on the job' as I encouraged and enabled children to remain in school, assembled clothing and school supplies, and managed other support services helping children stay in school. We also ran regular Christian camps during the school holidays.

For most of my young life, I had found myself in the position of a rescuer. I had done whatever it took to keep my brother and sister safe, and now, every time Helping Hands organized a camp, I brought Zarina and Yura along with me. We had so much fun together, and years later Yura told me those camps had helped to keep his heart soft in a rough environment.

Trauma can result in mental health issues that may not be obvious or easily diagnosed. All three of us had suffered trauma, and this affected the way we lived our lives. In my case, I had experienced a very real encounter with the presence of God, which completely changed the course of my life. This was followed by a period of healthy living in a loving environment during my teenage years. Zarina and Yura, however, did not have these things, and they suffered for it.

CHAPTER ELEVEN

BOTH MY BROTHER AND SISTER BECAME VICTIMS OF THE JUSTICE system in Tajikistan. Both were unjustly sent to prison for theft, both for minor crimes that in most developed countries would merely result in community service. It was common in Tajikistan for prisoners to receive disproportionate sentences. The theft of two bags of flour led to one prisoner receiving an eight-year sentence, compared to another engaged in drug trafficking that resulted in a two-year sentence only. One youth was sentenced to seven years in prison for stealing a single book from the city library. Later, this same youth was one of many killed during the uprising of April 1997.

The April riots began at the Khujand Men's Correctional Colony, with prisoners protesting the poor living conditions, the lack of medical care for the seriously ill, and the unreasonably long delays for those awaiting sentencing. At the time, between eight hundred and one thousand prisoners were housed in the overcrowded Khujand prison—twice the maximum number allowed.

It was in this volatile environment that, whilst still teenagers, Zarina and Yura were imprisoned amongst grown men and women, some of whom were genuine criminals. The trauma from this experience has left permanent scars on their lives. But their needless suffering could have been prevented if only they'd had someone to advocate on their behalf.

It was years later, however, when I finally learned the full extent of Zarina's tragic story from her own mouth:

"From a young age, we watched our mother prostitute herself to feed us so we could survive, but it was very difficult for me because we had a one-room apartment. I saw those men; I saw Mama being regularly abused by the men, and I saw it all with my own eyes. When I was between thirteen and fifteen years old, those same men began harassing me."

Zarina told me she ran away from home many times to get away from the men's constant badgering. She slept on roofs, in trees, and in basements, and whenever she slept on a roof, she would lift up the insulation and hide underneath so that no one would see her and rape her. Being a virgin woman in our country is of great importance—otherwise, you can never get married as you are considered 'used'. Losing our virginity was a heavy fear for us as young girls.

One night, Zarina climbed into our cousin's place through the balcony, as she was starving and needed money to buy food. Our cousin's husband caught her and beat her so badly that he broke her arm. The family called an ambulance, and a cast was put on her arm. "I will always remember those moments because they were so painful," she told me. "There was no one to protect me, no one to feed me, no one to take me in—not even family wanted to help."

When my sister was fifteen, she ran away from home and went to stay with her girlfriend, Feruza. Two years younger than Zarina, Feruza knew where they could get some food and maybe even some money. She took Zarina to the apartment of a man everyone called Mr. Bird because he kept a lot of birds in his house—he was obsessed with birds.

"Mr. Bird fed us a disgusting, watery soup," Zarina recalled, "but I drank it because I was hungry. Then Feruza told me to distract Mr. Bird while she slipped into the other room to search for his money."

Mr. Bird was kind and gentle with his birds, but it was well-known that he was a pervert and a paedophile. He would often lure in young girls who had run away from home, offering them food and a place to live, then raping them once they were in his apartment. But if a girl could stand up for herself, he wouldn't bother with her. Sure enough, he tried to make a move on Zarina.

"He started touching me. He was very strong, as he had once been a taekwondo fighter. He twisted my arms, but I pushed him off because I was strong too. I had survived on the streets and could look after myself."

Zarina ran out of the room and quickly found her friend. "Come on, now *you* go and distract him," she whispered to Feruza.

I've got to be quick, Zarina thought, and she began diligently searching for his money while Feruza took her turn distracting the man. Soon, Zarina's probing fingers found an envelope tucked behind one of the cages. She pulled it out quickly and then, remembering that Mr. Bird always searched girls leaving his apartment to make sure they didn't steal anything, she hid the envelope in the heel of her sock and stuffed her feet back into her shoes. As the two girls left, Mr. Bird searched them and found nothing. Outside on the street, Zarina bent down and removed her sock. She opened the envelope to show her friend the money that was inside.

"That's American money," Feruza said excitedly. "Hundred-dollar bills!" Zarina had never seen American money before, but now she had a wad of nearly three thousand dollars in her sock.

Feruza took charge. "We need to get far away from here—now. I have a family friend in Kanibadam City; we can stay there."

The two girls immediately took a bus to Kanibadam City, two hours away in northern Tajikistan, and went straight to the apartment of Feruza's family friend. When they knocked on the door, a man welcomed them in. As Feruza introduced Zarina, they could see he was watching boxing videos, with many of the clips being recordings of himself in prize-winning fights. "Come, sit down and enjoy this with me," he said. "Would you like a *suhoe vino*?" he added as they sat down.

People in Tajikistan aren't always familiar with wine, as vodka and beer are the cultural drinks. So Zarina didn't know what *suhoe vino*—a dry wine—was. She thought he was offering a juice that tasted like dried tomato; she didn't realize it was alcohol. Soon, the *suhoe vino* made her tipsy. Noting her reaction to the wine, their host whispered slyly, "Come, Zarina, I'll show you some of my boxing trophies in the other room."

Feruza stayed behind, watching the television. She had seen all the trophies before and wasn't interested. But Zarina went with their host to look at his awards lining the walls of the other room. The man shut the door behind them and started touching her. He was playful and laughing, but she suddenly understood what was happening.

"Please don't touch me," she begged him. "I'm a virgin—I'm only fifteen." But he quickly overpowered her, pushing her down onto the floor.

"Feruza!" Zarina cried out for help, and to her relief, she heard Feruza open the door. But the man yelled at the young girl, "Get out of here! We're fine."

"Okay," replied Feruza as she backed away and retreated.

Zarina began struggling and crying loudly, but the man forced her arms behind her and raped her. Finally, she managed to kick him hard, and she tore herself out of his grasp, running down the hall and into the bathroom. She locked the door behind her, and that's when she saw the blood streaming down her legs. Zarina was numb with anguish. *I can never be married now. Nobody will ever marry me because I'm used.*

Stricken with horror and grief, she found a blade under the bathroom sink and frantically slashed at her wrists. Then her attacker banged violently on the bathroom door, forcing it open and bursting inside. He froze in shock as he saw the blood spread all around the bathroom. Taking advantage of his surprise and distraction, Zarina ran for the apartment door with Feruza following her.

The two girls escaped the apartment and ran and ran. The blade had been blunt and my sister's injuries, while bloody, were not life-threatening. They found a public toilet where Zarina cleaned herself up, then they hurriedly boarded the bus back to Khujand.

Zarina collapsed gratefully once she had finally made it home, but in just a few hours, the district police and Mr. Bird arrived at the door. They had found Feruza, and she'd told them where Zarina lived, insisting, "I had nothing to do with this—it was all Zarina's idea! I just followed along with her."

Since Feruza was only thirteen, two years younger than my sister, she got away with her story. But Zarina, hurting and broken, was hauled away to a penal cell where she confessed to taking Mr Bird's money.

Our mother didn't go to the penitentiary with her youngest daughter, but Zarina didn't care. Mama was always cursing her and beating her anyway. And so, at fifteen years old, my little sister was convicted and imprisoned with real criminals—hardened adult women who treated her with indifference and brutality. With a sentence of four years, Zarina was released after two horrific years in jail due to her good behaviour because she was quiet and did not create trouble.

Desperate to find a job as soon as she was released, Zarina heard about a farm outside Moscow offering work. The farm supposedly boasted a large vegetable garden as well, where workers could gather vegetables to feed themselves. A sum of thirty thousand Russian rubles was promised, which was an unbelievable amount of money to a newly released ex-prisoner. Arrangements were made through a close friend of Zarina's, and a ticket to Moscow was even included in the deal.

"I was so trusting and so young," Zarina remembered. "Only seventeen and wearing a dirty cotton dress with my hair in braided pigtails."

Upon her arrival, Zarina was taken to an ugly apartment complex with broken glass, old cigarettes and cigar butts lying around. "I didn't like the look of it," Zarina told me later, "but I trusted my friend who had helped me secure this farm job, so I told myself I had no need to fear. But only moments later, I knew I had done a stupid thing."

Zarina entered the apartment to see cats everywhere and a big dog running around unchecked. Three women met her at the door, and as one took her passport, they told her she needed to quickly go and take a shower. "There's no time to talk," the woman hurried her along. "The client is coming."

What client? Zarina wondered. *Where is he coming from? What for?* She was still naively hopeful that her growing fears weren't about to become real.

After she had washed, the women gave Zarina a change of clothes. "I don't understand," she said to them desperately. "What aren't you telling me?" One of the women swore at her angrily. "If you do something wrong now, you'll have a problem later," she warned. "Just put on your underwear and stay in the kitchen."

"What am I going to do?" Zarina pushed back. "Prostitute myself?"

Instead of answering her question, another woman poured Zarina a glass of wine and thrust it towards her. "Talk less and drink this to get courage."

With a sinking heart, Zarina realized there was no way out. She had been caught in a trap, and now she would have to do whatever they told her. The client turned out to be a Tajik man, and from the lineup of young girls, he selected Zarina. *Perhaps he will help me escape,* she thought hopefully. Instead, she was pulled into an awful nightmare. Her fellow countryman was not at all interested in Zarina's problems, and he abused her and tormented her without remorse. She wept bitterly but endured it all.

Zarina had always been afraid something like this might happen to her, leaving her unable to get married and step into a secure future. But now she was living like our mother—alone and buried in the dark world of prostitution. What she had always feared was her new reality.

Look where money took me, Zarina thought to herself. *Is this where one ends up simply due to being poor?*

The abuse was awful, and Zarina suffered greatly. But then she found herself in the company of a Russian man. This man liked to talk and drink a lot, but he was not so interested in getting what he had paid for. No one else liked him because of that, but for Zarina, he was a welcome respite.

"We aren't allowed to drink in the bedroom," she told him on their first meeting.

"You can with me," the man winked. "With me, you can do everything—because I am the one with the money." He had a lot of money in his pocket and he asked Zarina to hide it for him. He also paid the woman in charge extra money for not giving him any trouble.

One evening, the Russian man took Zarina out to a restaurant. Usually, she wasn't allowed to leave the apartment, but he paid extra for her company that night. In the restaurant, far away from listening ears, Zarina told him her story of being brought to Russia on the false promise of farm work, only to end up a slave. Worse, her captors would only release her passport if she paid them forty thousand rubles. Immediately, the man rose from the table and went to a nearby ATM, where he withdrew some money. In an overwhelming act of benevolence, he retrieved my sister's passport and gave it back to her, having paid the fee in full. Zarina was overjoyed to find herself free, but once again she was alone on the streets, looking for work—this time in a foreign country.

When she met a Tajik man, despite all the horrors she'd been through, she longed to trust someone. This man helped her, letting her sleep in his car. She soon fell in love with him, and he took her to his apartment—but there he began to abuse her. Desperate to get out of Russia, Zarina stole as much of this man's money as she could find, returning to Tajikistan even more broken and world-weary than she had been when she left.

CHAPTER TWELVE

I AM INTIMATELY FAMILIAR WITH ZARINA'S STORY, YET MY HEART STILL aches deeply when I ponder her sufferings. I can't help but think of all the lost children who will never escape the traps of human trafficking and exploitation, and all the children and teenagers who, even now, are being tricked into leaving Tajikistan behind, unaware of the hell awaiting them on the other side. Before 1992, virtually no cases of women being trafficked from Tajikistan were reported. But ever since the dismantling of the Soviet Union, human trafficking has reached epidemic proportions.

In a world of poor economic prospects and increasing poverty, countless youth are attracted to the Russian Federation as a destination where salaries are far higher. Many of the victims of trafficking are young women, often with no higher education or job prospects, making it easy for traffickers to lure them with empty promises of genuine, well-paid jobs abroad.

Huge emigration numbers from Tajikistan into Russia are further complicating the situation, with men from rural villages going to Russia for work, leaving their women and children behind. Then, inevitably, those men remain in Russia, where wages are higher and life is easier; they then sever the tie with their wives, using the legitimate Muslim practice of announcing a divorce over the phone. They soon take a Russian wife, leaving their women and children abandoned in Tajikistan. If those families are left without sons, they turn to the daughters, sending them to Russia for work as soon as they turn eighteen. This practice is especially rife in rural areas where girls have little opportunity for education.

Sadly, what comes next is an all-too-common story: An eighteen-year-old girl in a rural village hears about the possibility of good work in Russia. She and her family raise money for an air ticket, usually by going into debt with the bank or a credit card. This creates further pressure as the high interest compounds, and what was originally a loan for one hundred dollars quickly becomes three hundred dollars. When the hopeful daughter lands at the local airport of her destination, she is easily identifiable because of her clothing and demeanour—she stands out as an uneducated, rural girl. The trafficking is well-organized, with someone taking a photo of the girl at the Tajik airport before she has left the country and sending her picture to a colleague in Russia who then waits for her to arrive. When the girl lands in Russia, most often in Moscow, the lookout will approach her with a quick offer. "Hey, you're here for work—we have a job for you! We can pay you in advance, five thousand rubles, and you can send that to your mother now."

The girl is astounded to find work so quickly. *This is awesome,* she thinks. She agrees to take the job, and often the trafficker will help her into a legitimate role, such as a cleaner or an unskilled factory worker. Once she's established and feeling secure, she is approached again. This time she is told, "You can earn even more, you know. Twice as much for less work . . ." and this is where she is introduced to sexual exploitation. She'll do it, she decides, *just this one time.* But she soon finds herself trapped and is sold on to a brothel.

It is difficult to determine just how many women have been trafficked out of Tajikistan, as the trafficking 'business' keeps a low profile. No official statistics are available, and victims are threatened to stay silent. Some victims are recruited by friends, relatives, or acquaintances, who offer them paid work abroad or talk about alleged 'opportunities' and show off newly purchased goods or property. This is probably what happened to my friend Yuliya.

'Second wave' recruitment occurs when trafficked women return home to snare other women. Often, this is the only way they are allowed to return home—by finding another young woman to replace them. There are also cases of young women being kidnapped off the streets, and this practice was already becoming increasingly common when I was still attending school.

In many cases, the traffickers arrange the woman's travel documents, visas and airline tickets, even outfitting them with new, smart clothing—as I had experienced when I was offered a 'job' delivering a package into Russia. If a woman does not have a passport or is underage, then a fraudulent passport is arranged. The price for a new passport ranges from one hundred to eight hundred US dollars, but as traffickers deal in US dollars, it's very easy for them to change Tajik somoni into US bills. There are currency exchange booths on almost every street intersection.

Freshly outfitted and with all the necessary documents in hand, the young women—and in some cases, young men—arrive at their destination only to have their passports taken from them. These are then retained by the traffickers to control their victims who are told they must work without wages until the travel expenses are paid off. In Zarina's case, she was informed it would cost her forty thousand rubles to buy her passport back. Victims are treated severely if they do not obey the rules, often subjected to violence or threats toward their families.

The government of Tajikistan does not currently comply with the minimum standards set in place to eliminate trafficking, although it reports making 'significant efforts' to be compliant. Due to my country's failure to provide evidence of increasing efforts to combat human trafficking, Tajikistan is on the 'Developing Nations Tier 2 Watchlist'. There have been very few trafficking convictions, despite the government training guards at Dushanbe Airport and along the border checkpoints, supposedly to identify traffickers and victims.

Both Zarina and Yuliya managed to escape their trafficked situations and return to Tajikistan, but they still suffered terribly. Their experiences mirror the stories of so many young women in Tajikistan, and it is my sincere longing and hope to change this tragic reality.

CHAPTER THIRTEEN

I'M AN ADVENTURER AT HEART, AND AT NEARLY EIGHTEEN I FOUND myself pondering something a Russian girl had said to me when I'd met her at the church I attended while living with Arthur and Larisa. Roksana had come to our city of Khujand in her second year of Bible college in Moscow to complete her student missionary experience. Her visit also coincided with the 9/11 event in the USA.

Big things are happening in the world God, I had prayed at the time. *Something is happening, and I do not know what to do. I don't want to just sit around here and do nothing. Jesus, please use me; I want to do everything you want me to do, instead of sitting around while people need help.*

Roksana had left an impression on me. She encouraged me to come to Moscow, and an idea began to grow in my mind. I dreamed of moving to Moscow, studying at the Bible school, and becoming equipped to help people in the same way Roksana was training to do. I would have left Tajikistan much sooner, but I was not legally allowed to travel on my own outside the country until I was of age.

As soon as I turned eighteen, I applied for the Bible school in Moscow. The college accepted my application, and I quit the choreography course at the local college in Khujand and booked myself a flight to Moscow.

In my pocket, I had the equivalent of fifty US dollars; in my hand, a small suitcase of clothing. Many of my friends and family thought this trip was a crazy idea, but I held on to Roksana's words of encouragement. She had agreed to meet me at Domodedovo airport, and I would stay with her and her mother in central Moscow until I found a place to rent for myself.

Roksana let me sleep in her room, and she and her mother generously shared their food with me. On my first night in Moscow, I woke up restless, thinking about the big move I'd made. Tossing and turning, I eventually found my way back to my dreams, but the deafening city sounds broke into my sleep. Cars honked noisily, engines roared to life, voices exclaimed loudly, and a truck rumbled past shaking all the street-side windows. Lights were flicking on and off in the neighboring apartments.

"Welcome to Moscow, Marina. The city that never sleeps," Roksana laughed.

The first few months were exciting; everything was big and new, but I also found it very uncomfortable as everything was so loud. Khujand City was a quiet little town by comparison, but in Moscow, the constant hum of activity never stopped. The bright lights at night, the loud metro trains, the non-stop roar of sound—it all affected me profoundly, and I slowly developed what turned out to be chronic fatigue. I was always tired. Every time I got onto the Metro and sat down, I would instantly fall asleep. I had to devise clever ways to hang onto my bag carefully to make sure I wasn't robbed, and I missed my stop on many occasions. It was difficult to adjust to my new life and I ended up simply trying to survive, much as I had in the life I'd left behind.

Eventually, as winter arrived, I found a casual job and a single room to rent—but in order to afford the rent, I had to share it with three others. Moscow's winters are brutal, with the daily temperature usually hovering around fourteen degrees Fahrenheit (minus ten degrees Celsius). I was colder than I'd ever been before. The icy winds sliced straight through my light spring jacket—the only one I had—and chilled me to the bone.

From early morning to late afternoon, I studied hard, then hurried to my job which I worked late into the evening. My wages had to cover my Bible school fees, train tickets, rent, and some simple food, and I only slept four or five hours a night.

One of my most precious treasures from that time was a letter that Mama wrote to me. I know she loved me, and this letter that she wrote— the only letter I ever received from her—spoke volumes regarding her deep concern for me. I have no cherished items or mementoes from my childhood—no toys, no clothing. The only gifts I have from my mother are a scarf and the letter which she wrote for me in Russian, while I was far from home and alone in a foreign country.

Apart from my joy over receiving news from home, I was touched by her care which was obvious in her words:

"I love you dearly and long to see you. I worry about you and pray that everything will work out for you. We have received your letter and photos. It looks like you have gotten thinner. You haven't told me that life is hard for you, but I will pray for you, my darling, that you will always have hope ... Thank you for your help, but please do not send any more money—I am managing ... Do not let your spirit down. Take care of yourself. It is my deepest desire that you will be alright."

The entire letter was a surprise, as Mama did not normally speak to me this way. The words she had penned were gentle, and I could feel her love for me. Her care and hope lifted my heart in a time of lonely struggle.

As a Tajik citizen, I strictly needed an official Moscow visa to allow me to live and work there. However, in order for me to become registered for this, a citizen from Moscow would need to register me at their home address. I often wondered why Roksana's mother didn't offer to do this. Maybe it was because this registration meant she would have to provide a home address for me for a long time, but her invitation to me had been for a brief initial stay only.

It was impossible to find someone to register me, so I moved from job to job so that the police wouldn't notice me and ask for my registration. I worked as a cleaner, a nanny, a salesperson in an open-air market or at the mall—I even took on a job handing out advertising brochures on the street.

I was always hungry, as these short-term jobs were not well paid. I never had enough money to buy adequate food, so I made do with bread, instant noodles and occasionally some milk. I was hardly ever able to buy fresh fruit or vegetables, and my poor diet, as well as chronic sleep deprivation, meant I was gradually becoming more and more unwell.

One night, on my way to work after a Bible school class, I was hit by a wave of sickness while traveling on the Metro. I forced myself to rest on a seat without going to sleep, and when my stop was announced, I stepped carefully off the train. I walked across to the station wall, leaned on it briefly, then gently slid down and fainted. No one approached to ask if I needed help—normal in Moscow—and I found myself lying on the cold, hard ground, unable to get up. I took a few deep breaths and when I had recovered enough to stand, I began the half-mile walk to my kiosk at the mall, where I worked as a salesperson handing out samples of Nivea face cream.

Cautious, I was always on the alert during this walk. The police made a fortune-hunting down outsiders like me and making money from us in the form of bribes. I lived in fear of the authorities. If they stopped me on the street, my papers were not in order and my story was probably not good enough to prevent me from being arrested unless I was able to bribe them—something I could not afford.

The next night, as I walked to the mall from the station again, a man approached me. It was dark and cold, and he shoved a registration document at me. "You'll need some identification if you're going to work in Moscow," he said.

How does he know I don't have any ID? The paper was probably fake. I'd been warned that many agencies could produce registration documents for a price, but they were usually identified by the police as being counterfeit. "No thanks," I replied. While people like me often paid for the necessary papers, I didn't have the money to buy either papers or bribes.

Later that week, the police caught me out. I had no money to give them, so they put me in jail with the other people they'd caught that day—all of whom were older men. At the end of the day I was released, as they did not want to deal with the deportation paperwork.

It was a huge effort for me to finish my first year of Bible school, and I did not intend to do a second. I found the teaching unrelatable and difficult to comprehend, and I did not do well in many of my classes, especially theology and evangelism. At nearly nineteen, I was still young and insecure. I hated talking to people on the streets, especially as most of them were hostile and rude. Constant hunger and sleep deprivation did not help, and I just wanted to sleep every time I stopped moving and sat down.

◆ ◆ ◆

APART FROM MY OWN TROUBLES, MY HEART WAS ALSO HEAVY FOR MY sister Zarina. She had returned to Tajikistan after being trafficked to Russia, and she went back home to live with Mama again. Still too trusting, she met a man and soon became pregnant. Unfortunately, this man did not want to be bothered with Zarina or a baby. Mama called our cousin to come over and handed Zarina some money. "Marina has sent me $50 to give you for an abortion," she told my sister. "Here . . ."

"She also said you should get rid of the baby," our cousin insisted. "Come, I'll take you to see Dr. Rosa."

I often reflect that if only we'd had access to cell phones, the message Zarina received might have been different. But reaching my family at any time was difficult, and the fact that I was always moving from one place to the other only made it harder. The only way I could get in touch was by phoning my Mom's next-door neighbor, who had a home phone. Even so, calls were expensive, and whenever I hung up the phone, it grieved me to realize how much was left unsaid. I thought about when Zarina was trafficked. I had no idea she was in Russia. When I later learned that my sister was in the same city as me and I'd hadn't known, it broke my heart. Now, she was pregnant with her first baby and she thought I was encouraging her to have an abortion. *If only I could have talked with Zarina herself.* Instead, Zarina went along with our cousin to the doctor's rooms.

When she met with the pair, Dr. Rosa reprimanded our cousin: "You've already had at least twenty abortions—and now you want to put this little sister under the knife?"

Our cousin ignored the doctor's comment and demanded Zarina get rid of the baby. That same week, Zarina had the abortion.

Afterwards, Zarina learned our cousin had lied about me sending them money for an abortion. She told me that when she underwent the abortion, she was already five months pregnant. "I felt like they were cutting me inside and taking my baby out in pieces."

◆ ◆ ◆

"Oh God, I've just found out. I don't know what to think. I don't even know what to say to you. I'm just sitting here weeping—the pain is indescribable. Zarina is only seventeen, only two years younger than I am. Her baby in the womb was five months old. There was a heartbeat. God, please help her, forgive her, do something. Father, you promised me in your word, "Believe in the Lord Jesus, and you will be saved, you and your household." I want my family to know you and trust you."

When I was fourteen, I had watched a painful documentary about abortion. Ever since, my heart had ached for the unborn children who were murdered, and for their mothers who thought they had no other choice. Now my little sister was one of those mothers.

◆ ◆ ◆

TOWARDS THE END OF MY YEAR IN MOSCOW, I BEGAN TO EXPERIENCE intense dreams at night—dreams that slowly changed the posture of my heart towards Mama. I was still very angry and resentful towards her; I could not understand why she had abused us as children, or the choices she'd made with prostitution and drinking.

But these recurring dreams had me in my mother's body; I was my Mama, experiencing all the abuse and suffering of her life. Every morning I woke up around three o'clock, weeping with the intensity of her pain. These dreams continued for several weeks, then stopped as abruptly as they had started.

By the end of this experience, all my thoughts and assumptions about Mama had been completely undone. A deep love and empathy for her began to form in my heart, and I made up my mind: *One day, and it's going to be very soon, I'm going to return home and connect deeply with her and help her in some way.*

Despite the difficulties of my life in Moscow, I developed some strong friendships that carried me through the tough times. I still kept in touch with Rune and Kari in Norway, and eventually, I told them I was not doing well at Bible school. I had never been able to ask for help or share my problems, but by this point, I was in great distress. They wrote back with an unexpected invitation: "Would you like to come and visit us in Norway?"

It had been several years since I'd lived with them, and the baby girl they'd had since then would be nearly three years old. I suddenly felt a deep longing to be in their safe and loving company again, and it was with great hope that I began the process of applying for a visa to visit Norway.

CHAPTER FOURTEEN

VERY LAST BIT OF MONEY I HAD WENT TO BUYING TICKETS—TRAIN, bus and ferry—that would take me through Russia to the border of Finland and then on to Sweden. Here, Rune would meet me at the Norwegian border and drive me to their home near Moss, in the south of Norway. Once all my travel expenses had been arranged, I was left with absolutely nothing to put towards food and accommodation for the three-day journey. I was only nineteen years old and not brave enough to ask my friends for help, so I set out with my tickets and no other means of cash or payment for anything else. I traveled all night on the train from Moscow to St. Petersburg, where I boarded a tourist bus that took me to the Russian-Finnish border.

It was here that my journey took a turn for the worse when the bus pulled in at the checkpoint on the Russian side. A border control officer entered the bus and carefully checked our passports. He abruptly ordered me off the bus, declaring I had produced a forged passport and visa, and waved the bus to continue on without me. Meanwhile, I was locked in a room enclosed with floor-to-ceiling panels of glass. I had no way of communicating with anyone, and I was constantly watched by people hovering on the other side of the glass panes. It was like being in a terrarium in a zoo.

Despondent, I sat alone in that room for several hours. I hadn't eaten anything for over a day and a half and had little to drink. Eventually, the stomach cramps caused such agony that I ended up doubling over in pain and lying down on the floor. When a man stepped into the room to interrogate me, I had enough presence of mind to explain, "I've got another passport."

"Well, give it to me," he replied curtly. "Don't waste my time."

As a Tajik citizen, I was issued with two passports: one for internal travel and one for international travel. The Russian border control officer had not asked me for my internal Tajik passport, and, in the confusion and shock of being pulled off the bus, I had not thought of offering it to him to validate my story. Fortunately, my internal passport proved I had not forged anything and helped to clarify the situation.

The border control officers still didn't seem entirely convinced that my Norwegian visa was legitimate, but they looked over my paperwork again, stamped my passport, and let me through. One of the officers briskly walked me outside, pointing me in the direction of the Finnish border. Far away in the distance, I could just make out the simple border hut of that country. The Russian officer left me alone to make my own way on foot, but I was still suffering excruciating stomach pain and looked a sorry sight as I hobbled onwards, bent over like an old woman and dragging my suitcase behind me. I had walked some distance before a friendly Russian couple pulled their vehicle over and offered me a lift for the last three miles.

In contrast to Russia's suspicion, the officers at the Finnish checkpoint were welcoming and kind. They knew something of my situation as the bus driver had notified them of my plight when he drove through. After verifying my identity and my visa, one of the officers gently asked if I had any friends or family in Finland who could collect me from the border station.

"This is the phone number of Rune and Kari Borgso, but they're in Norway," I replied, exhausted. I was grateful when the officer took matters into his own hands and contacted Rune, letting him know what had happened to cause me to be left behind by my bus.

Then I remembered something else. "I have the phone number of the Lux-Express bus company that I was traveling with. Is that any use?" I offered.

A quick phone call to Lux-Express and the driver of my previous bus was contacted. The Finnish officer then approached the occupants of another car passing through the checkpoint: "Would you mind dropping this young lady off at the bus stop in Kyminlinna as you pass through? She can catch up with her bus there as it will be due at that stop later today."

The couple in the car kindly agreed to drive me to the bus stop, although it was quite a distance from the border crossing. By now I was dehydrated as well as hungry and exhausted, and once I was safely inside their vehicle, I quickly fell fast asleep. The couple gently woke me as we pulled into the bus station, sending me off with a bottle of water and a legendary Finnish cinnamon roll.

And there was my bus. I stepped up into the large transport vehicle, and as soon as I entered, the passengers erupted into loud clapping and cheering. Everyone on the bus was relieved to see me and happy that I had managed to reconnect. With some difficulty, I found my seat. I was exhausted from the ordeals of the day, and I didn't care about the rest of the trip at all—I just wanted to stay put. I soon fell asleep again, feeling grateful for all the kind people who had cared enough to notice me and who now kept an eye on me as I rested.

Four hours later, we reached the Finnish ferry terminal where I boarded a ferry for the trip across the Gulf of Bothnia and into Sweden. On the Swedish side of the Gulf, I climbed into a second bus for the five-hour journey that would take me right across Sweden to the Norwegian border—the final border checkpoint. My passport and visa were in order, and I sat down to wait for Rune to arrive. I had no money to buy any food at all, and all I could think about was that huge cinnamon roll so kindly given to me. I longed for another.

When Rune stepped into the waiting room, in my hazy state, he seemed almost unreal. But I was so grateful to see him that I quickly put aside how tired, traumatized, and hungry I was. His warm smile and fatherly embrace melted away my distress, and he shared with me how miraculous the timing was that he could collect me from the Norwegian border checkpoint. Rune and the pastors of his church were driving back from a conference, and their journey had them traveling right through the place where I had ended up after several days of arduous travel. The group took me to a nearby café before we set off on our drive for the last leg home.

"Tell us what's been happening for you, Marina," encouraged Rune after I'd eaten and drunk. What a comfort it was for me to speak freely with people who loved me and cared for me, who knew me.

Rune and Kari lived near Moss, a coastal town in southern Norway, and it was late by the time Rune and I arrived at their house. The three children were in bed, but Kari was waiting up for us. I was flooded with joy seeing her again, and she welcomed me with so much love and excitement that I immediately felt at home. I was exhausted on every level, but now I also felt hopeful for the future. Kari fussed over me, giving me more food and making sure I had everything I needed for the night. Then she ushered me to a room which had been beautifully set up for my private use during my stay. I fell into bed with a heart full of gratitude and love for these wonderful people and their friendship and care that seemed to know no bounds.

CHAPTER FIFTEEN

EVEN THOUGH GOD HAD BEEN HEALING ME ON A SPIRITUAL LEVEL, I began experiencing various physical problems resulting from my lifestyle in Moscow that had exacerbated the trauma from my past. The continual lack of sleep and poor nutrition, combined with constant stress, had left me exhausted, but it wasn't until I arrived in Norway that I began to realize just how bone-weary I truly was.

One day, I jumped on Kari's bicycle and headed towards the tiny beach. The children had shown me this magical place, and it had become a perfect spot to sit and think. The pathway was damp and mossy, and the spruce trees, their tall trunks straight and graceful, looked down on me from high above as I pedaled beneath them. Five minutes later, I caught a glimpse of the water, and soon my gravelly little beach came into view, the huge walls of the fjord soaring upward behind it. I carefully laid the bike down on the stones and picked my way across the rocks to find a perch. But as I sat in peaceful silence, my thoughts seemed weighed down by the exhaustion that clung heavily to me. *I feel so tired all the time. Oh, why can I not settle and be happy?*

Rune and Kari's home was quiet and safe. I had plenty of food and a beautiful house to return to each day. No noisy Metro was clogging up my ears. No busy highways. No walking around on constant alert, wary of police. The natural environment all around me in Norway was exceptionally soothing, yet somehow my body seemed incapable of proper rest.

The exhaustion presented itself in odd ways. Unable to sleep at night, I got into the habit of reading all night and into the early hours of the morning, then sleeping all day—if the day allowed it. However, that was rarely an option, so I simply 'existed' throughout the long daylight hours, feeling groggy and tired. The cycle repeated itself with grim perseverance. I was not lazy—I simply could not regulate my sleeping patterns which had become so imbalanced. With the lack of proper rest taking its toll, I felt the dark cloud taking over again, sucking the life and joy from me relentlessly.

Rune had organized for me to learn Norwegian at the local school, and I also took on a small job cleaning part of the school while the janitor was away. This gave me a little pocket money. We'd all expected that my living with Rune, Kari, and their young children would be easy and comfortable for everyone, but it wasn't. I joined their church, I was included in family outings, I spent time with the children, but none of us imagined how difficult our shared life was going to get.

Years later, when we reflected together on my time with them in Norway, we realized that I had spent only a couple of months total living in their home in Tajikistan. Rune and Kari had not been aware of just how much I was affected by the extensive trauma I'd suffered as a child, and they remembered me as a lively teenager, a good communicator, and a bright and cheerful presence. They had never seen me hurting so deeply that I had to shut down, and they were not initially aware of the depression that was causing me to react in ways that weren't loving and kind.

I was so broken that I was unable to act normally. I did not know how to be part of a loving family, or how to give and receive love. In addition to my inner turmoil, the thoughts of my family's problems drained me. I felt powerless; I was unable to help them financially, nor could I communicate with them easily. My family did not have a phone, and an occasional landline call was expensive. Every now and then I called their neighbor, asking her to get in touch with Mama for me and to give me news of my brother and sister.

◆ ◆ ◆

ONE AFTERNOON, ZARINA CALLED ME UNEXPECTEDLY. THE ABORTION that my cousin had forced her into had shattered her world.

"I hated the whole world after that," she told me. "I hated everyone around me, and I wouldn't talk to anyone. I came home, prayed, and asked God for forgiveness. I asked him to give me one last chance because I had been told I wouldn't be able to have any more children after that abortion. I didn't care who the father of this next baby would be, I just kept asking God to bless my womb and give me a child."

Zarina wanted to be loved, and she wanted a child. Then she met Bakhadur. She told me that they did not love each other, and they hadn't lived together as a couple. But, to her great joy, Zarina became pregnant again. However, Bakhadur and Mama combined forces, demanding that Zarina go to the doctor for a second abortion. But as she sat miserably on the bus taking her to the doctor's rooms, a voice in her head stopped her: "I blessed your womb, and now you're going to kill again?" Right then and there, Zarina made up her mind—she would not have this abortion. Bakhadur was indifferent to the pregnancy, and when he heard of her decision, he refused to allow Zarina to speak about it to him again. As for our mother, she cursed Zarina, driving her out of the home.

My heart ached for my sister and her innocent child. "I will do everything I can for you," I promised her. "I will help you with your baby. I will not leave you." Together, we chose a name for her little baby boy: David.

◆ ◆ ◆

I ACHED TO SEE MY FAMILY AGAIN. AFTER A YEAR OF LIVING WITH RUNE and Kari in Norway, and financially supported by our church in Moss, I was able to plan a visit home to Tajikistan.

After landing at the airport in Dushanbe, I traveled on to Khujand by bus. I felt numb and impassive as I watched the landscape rolling by—city buildings, rural Tajik houses, then the beautiful but rugged mountains which took me up to their majestic heights and finally led down into Khujand. I would be staying with Arthur and Larisa, who had offered to host me while I visited Mama. They knew the 'shutdown' version of me, and I knew I'd be safe to ride the waves in their home.

Mama, Yuri and Zarina were very happy to see me. Mama had been anticipating my trip, as her neighbor had passed on my message informing her of my upcoming visit.

Oh, she's lost so much weight, I thought sadly as soon as I saw her. *She looks so much older.*

I'd brought lots of photos with me so that I could share a little about my life in Norway with my mother. As she sorted through them she asked, "Can I keep these?"

"No," I replied, probably a bit harshly.

Why on earth did I say no? My reactions were confusing, even to me. How insensitive I was; how shut down and detached I must be. I loved Mama deeply, but I treated her distantly. Looking back, I realize now that underneath it all was my deep-rooted fear of being hurt again. I did not know that trauma most often expresses itself in anger, nor did I understand the complexities of the loss and grief associated with long-term childhood trauma. All I knew was that kindness did not come naturally to me. Part of my journey towards healing would see me learning to *choose* kindness, even when my inner reaction might be the opposite. I would come to learn that love is a choice, and even today, I still have to work hard sometimes to choose love. But at the time of my visit, the tumultuous history between Mama and me kept us apart and prevented us from being vulnerable and intimate as mother and daughter.

◆ ◆ ◆

I WAS TWENTY-ONE WHEN I RETURNED TO NORWAY AFTER VISITING Tajikistan, and it quickly became evident that I could not live with Rune and Kari any longer. It was Rune who spoke with me gently but firmly, saying what we all knew to be true.

"Marina, Kari and I feel that, while we're raising our young family, we just don't have any extra energy left in us to be able to help you anymore."

I could understand their struggle to cope with my challenging health and wildly fluctuating moods, but once again, I found myself stepping out alone into an unknown future.

CHAPTER SIXTEEN

ITH RUNE AND KARI'S ASSISTANCE, I MOVED AN HOUR AWAY to Oslo, which turned out to be a better living situation for all of us. Rune had organized a room where I could live rent-free in exchange for cleaning the office area in the same building. In addition, I took on other cleaning jobs which covered the cost of basic food—mostly oats, milk, and some bread. I lived as cheaply as I could, saving hard so I could send money to Zarina for the care of her baby.

I began to think about my own future too, pondering questions that I had not been able to consider until now. *Could I really have choices? Could I ever get out of this lifestyle of struggle that was all too familiar to me?* My schooling had been neglected and interrupted by poverty and strife, and it truly was a gift when I discovered a Russian-speaking high school in the area where I was living. I applied to finish my high school diploma, and even though this school had been set up for Russian-speaking families who had been posted to Oslo for work, they accepted me and even welcomed me as a student.

High school in Oslo, and learning once again in my own language, was such fun for me. It didn't matter that I was a few years older than the other attendees. Our class was small—about ten students—and we all became good friends. I enjoyed the hour-long walk to school each day, admiring the Royal Palace and passing through the most beautiful graveyard I've ever seen. This cemetery was not like the ones I remember from home, which made me feel scared and sad. Graves in Khujand are set amongst the bare rocks of the mountainside with no flowers or trees, but this graveyard was like a park. Sprawling lawns were dotted with colorful flowers and elegant trees, the whole place overflowing with lush growth. As I made my way through the cemetery, I looked over the tombstones, noting people's names, their dates of birth and death, and the words their loved ones had written about them. I wondered about these people—who they were and what kind of lives they had led.

By the time I landed at the Royal Palace, my school was only a further ten minutes beyond. The front of the place boasted a huge public garden, and I often stopped to watch people meandering the garden paths. I could see through the massive gates into the palace gardens, and I would look carefully to see if I could spot any members of the royal family enjoying their own private greenery.

Almost everything about my schooling in Norway was in stark contrast to my schooling experiences in Khujand. Back home, I'd had the option of two routes to walk to school. One was significantly shorter, wending its way through construction sites, but you had to watch out for the man who liked to hide and then unexpectedly expose himself to a child passing through on their way to school. The shortcut also meant cutting through a deserted alley, and I sometimes walked that route when I was in a hurry to get home.

Once, as I ran alone through the narrow alley, an older boy from school attacked me from behind, attempting to rape me. He was much stronger than I, and for a moment, I was paralyzed with fear. But my anger kicked in, and I grabbed at a loose rock on the ground, hitting his head with such ferocity I could have killed him. He ran away, leaving me shaking for the rest of the day. I had a good cry, but I never shared the story with Mama, even though the incident had scared me so badly that it shook me up for days afterwards. That was the last time I ever took the shortcut.

Another difference between my two learning environments was that, at school in Khujand, if I caused any trouble the whole class would follow me. One of my favorite teachers understood that if she made peace with me, she made peace with the whole class.

"Marina," she said one day, "just so you know—I'll give you a good grade if you can just be good."

I agreed immediately. Wow, what an awesome deal! Yeah, I'll be good. And soon there was peace in the class.

In Khujand, our Russian literature teacher—who loved her subject dearly and who had not survived the war just to be messed around by a bunch of students—yelled at us often. She told us we were spoilt, ranting about how she'd had to eat dead horses during the war. We were all from poor families, but war is another level of deprivation. I didn't like hearing her stories, and I didn't make any effort to participate in her classes.

In contrast, my teachers in Norway were amazing. They were kind, interested in the students, and they were passionate about their subjects. They ignited a joy of learning in the students. I was older now, and my life was peaceful. For me, studying became a joy.

When I eventually left the Russian school in Oslo, the teachers and students created a large photo book for me, filling it with images of our time together, and lots of beautiful, encouraging messages. To this day, I look back on my time there as a really special experience.

◆ ◆ ◆

LIVING ALONE AT TWENTY-ONE WAS GOOD FOR ME. WITH EACH PASSING day I was able to relax more; my internal struggles no longer overflowed to impact everyone else. My earnings didn't allow much money for food or clothes, but that didn't matter to me. I was happy.

One day after school, I visited the most amazing library I'd ever seen—the Oslo Public Library. When I came across the Lord of the Rings books in English, I had an idea. A friend had given me an audio player, and I approached the librarian with a request: "May I borrow the hard copy books as well as the audiobooks?" I explained what I wanted to do, and she enthusiastically agreed, "Yes, of course."

Thus began many, many hours of enjoyment, as I found myself engrossed in the intrigue and excitement of these books. I was fascinated by this series, but Lord of the Rings gave me more than just happy hours of reading. I listened to the audiobook at the same time as I followed the text in the books, and in this way, I learned to read and write English. Lost in the wonder of this tale, my ability to understand and speak English increased exponentially.

As I relaxed into my new life, I fell in love with Oslo. There were lots of opportunities to do all sorts of interesting activities, and my interest in dance and choreography was further ignited when I joined the local free dance classes run by a Christian woman. Walking around the city, I savored the delicious smells of the famous Oslo Fjord prawns being cooked at street stalls and watched the changing of the guards as I walked past the Royal House.

I made good friends in Oslo, though I still preferred to keep people at a distance. I felt safer this way, deciding my issues would impact others less if I didn't let them get too close. *If people get to know me better, they will be affected by my brokenness,* I thought. Even though I loved Jesus deeply and had changed so much, I still held deep pain within my soul. I carried that 'disconnection' with me for many years, and even now, being vulnerable with others is not easy.

John and Ann Kristin from the church had befriended me soon after I moved to Oslo. They often invited me to stay at their place on weekends and during school holidays. Kindness and love developed a special bond between Ann and me. We took long walks together, praying and talking, and she became the close friend I so desperately needed. Gentle and kind, Ann never criticized me or tried to change me. I felt so accepted in her presence, and her kindness impacted me so deeply that I still feel the effects to this day.

John and Ann could see I was happy in Oslo, and they wanted to help me stay in Norway and attend university. This encouraged me greatly. University could prove to be the once-in-a-lifetime opportunity that would lift me out of poverty and free me from a future that lacked possibility. I began looking forward to the end of my school year, anticipating a bright new life in Oslo.

The winter drew to a satisfying close, but in early spring, I received a disturbing phone call from Yura. "Mama's very, very sick," he sobbed. My heart dropped. Yura still relied on me as the oldest sister—both he and Zarina did—to care for our family.

I knew I needed to go home. It could be the last time I would ever see Mama.

God, you showed me that one day my relationship with my mama would change, and I'd be able to do something wonderful to help her. Could this be the time?

In that moment, I set aside my hopes for the chance at a life in Oslo, instead turning my thoughts to how I might pay for a ticket to fly home. I owned very little and had only two hundred American dollars in savings. The church I had been going to with Rune and Kari had raised support for me the last time I visited my family, but their pastor had just left, and the new pastor didn't know me. I was no longer a member of their church, and he did not want to raise support for an outsider's trip to Tajikistan. I was at a loss, not knowing what to do or how to get home. Then, out of their unending kindness, John and Ann paid for my air ticket.

Forced to wait a few weeks before my trip, I held onto hope for my family. During those long weeks of uncertainty, I wrote in my journal:

My dear friend, Jesus, please help me to restore my connection with my family—without their happiness, mine will never be complete. My dream is that we become a true family, just like you intended us to be. I know you can do that. I love and trust you, and I am grateful for my siblings and my mama.

Finally, one month after I'd heard of Mama's illness, I boarded a plane for Tajikistan with no plan to return to Norway. I was twenty-one. I had left home with nothing, and now I was returning with nothing. I was going back to pain and brokenness, and I had nothing to offer my family.

CHAPTER SEVENTEEN

A S I TRAVELED BACK TO MY HOMELAND, MY THOUGHTS LINGERED on my two foster families—Larissa and Arthur, and Rune and Kari. I had never realized what a big 'yes' they offered when they took me in. Both couples had been in their early thirties with children of their own, yet they had graciously accepted the challenge of a teenager from a very difficult background, encircling me with their love. My mama and my brother and sister had never been surrounded by love, and as the passing hours drew me ever closer to home, my heart ached for my broken family.

◆ ◆ ◆

SILENCE HUNG HEAVILY IN THE AIR, DESPITE THE TWO OF US BEING IN the room—Mama lying in agony on her old bed in our old state-owned apartment, and me fresh and well after my active life in Oslo. For my mother, nothing had changed, and my ability to connect with her hadn't changed either.

"Get me another vodka, Marina," she murmured.

"Oh Mama, this won't help you." I had been warned that her liver was shutting down and she was in severe pain. She was bleeding internally, but we had no money to take her to the hospital, no morphine tablets or any painkillers at all. We could only take turns to nurse her in bed as she lay ashen and silent, drinking vodka to allay the pain. There was nothing I could do for her except be with her.

Later in the afternoon, a knock sounded at the door. Our neighbor had come to sit with Mama so that I could go to my friend's apartment to rest. Thinking she was asleep, I quietly made my way to the bedroom door, when I heard her softly call my name: "Marina . . ."

I turned to see what she wanted. "I love you," she whispered. Those were rare words to hear spoken aloud in our family, and I smiled at her gratefully.

With Mama's declaration of love, happy childhood memories came flooding back, and my heart leaned into them to see where they would take me. I remembered days when she gently woke us for school with breakfast ready—oatmeal, or sweet tea and bread made with many grains, or very occasionally, eggs. On some hot summer evenings, she would take the hose outside and spray us with water, Mama laughing as we giggled and jumped around. I still remember how much fun we had, screaming in delight, running and dodging back and forth for a long time until we were soaked with water and happiness.

My favorite days were when we went to the river. Mama would pack a picnic and take all three of us, and we would swim until we were freezing. She'd called for us to get out of the water and come and get warm, but we would protest loudly, our lips blue and our bodies shivering as we shouted, "We're not *c-c-c-c-c-oooold!*" Still laughing, we eventually clambered out to be greeted by Mama unpacking the picnic—our favorite food in the world—*kulcha,* traditional rounds of Tajik bread with fresh watermelon.

I remembered Mama helping me to memorize a poem for school by turning it into a song—I still remember that poem. And when we were sick, she cared for us. Once, I fainted in the street and Mama carried me home, carefully washing me and looking after me until I had recovered.

That afternoon, as I left our kind neighbor with Mama and walked along the noisy street to my friend's apartment, I pondered how, despite the hell on earth that had been her life, Mama had still found some capacity to love and delight in us, her precious children.

◆ ◆ ◆

THE NEXT MORNING, MAMA HAD TAKEN A TURN FOR THE WORSE. YURA and I phoned the emergency department at the hospital, then gently carried her down the flight of stairs and into the waiting ambulance. The drive to the hospital was rough, and Mama was in so much pain that she went into shock. The hospital staff did little for her, and we could not pay for the expensive pain medication.

At the age of forty-three, Mama knew that she was slipping away. She had lived with pain all her life, and now she was dying in agony. It was traumatizing for us as her children to watch our mother go in such distress. I felt terribly guilty over not being able to help ease her suffering in her final moments. Even my deeply held hopes and prayers hadn't made a difference. How I wish now that I could turn back time and at least pay for the pain medication that would have allowed her to pass with some measure of comfort.

We didn't hold the funeral that Russians and Tajiks would traditionally expect. Normally, one would keep the body of the deceased in the home for a while after death. Family and friends would come and bring food, and everyone would grieve together and eat together, processing the loss and supporting those most closely affected. We three children didn't have any of that. We buried Mama the same day she died, as we could only afford a simple burial. A few friends helped make the burial arrangements for us, as we were in too much shock and pain to manage the details.

I held Zarina and Yura tightly in my arms as soundless, gut-wrenching cries ravaged my whole body, silent tears streaming down my cheeks. Mama's death crushed me, and I genuinely felt as though part of my own heart had died that day. We watched her casket being lowered into the ground, and as the rough earth was heaped over her grave, for the first time we realized how alone we were. We had no one. I knew then that Mama had loved us deeply. Her love may not have been vocal or readily available on the surface, but she had expressed it in the many sacrifices she had made so that we, her children, could live.

After we buried our mother, we walked slowly back to Mama's apartment. My heart was overwhelmed with the trauma of Mama's final days of suffering and her subsequent death. I hadn't been able to connect with her, and now all my hopes for her were lost. All my hopes for myself were gone too. I had family to care for—my brother, my sister and her one-year-old son David. I had returned to Tajikistan with no money, and I possessed no skills that would make me employable. Only recently, I had been living a different life, buoyed by hope and a newly found determination to make a future for myself. But now I was falling back into the darkness.

I BEGAN TO DRINK MAMA'S VODKA. ONLY WHEN I WAS DRUNK COULD I release the intensity of my built-up emotions. I would drink on my own until I was able to weep. As the days went on and my grief slowly poured out, somehow within my darkness, an almost imperceptible spark of hope was ignited. We couldn't stay here in Mama's apartment anymore—the pain was too much to bear—and I knew I had to find a job.

A tiny studio apartment with no furniture became available nearby, and I persuaded Yura and Zarina that we should all move and then look for jobs. We bought a child's bed for David, but Zarina, Yura, and I slept on the floor. We brought some old items with us from the apartment and neighbors gave us some old bedding.

Yura soon found a job selling pastries on the streets, and Zarina cleaned houses whenever she could. An internet café had taken me on as an operator, signing people in and making sure they were allocated a computer. But even with our various jobs, we barely made enough to pay for rent and basic food. It was as if we'd fallen right back into our old life. The three of us were in survival mode again, all working hard and sharing the care of little David, with no room for emotions and no understanding of how to process our grief and anger. We never talked to each other about our pain. We simply pushed on with the heavy task of getting through each day.

One evening, as little David slept, I read a book out loud to the others. I had recently begun Dostoyevsky's *Crime and Punishment*, and now I was reading from chapter four where Rodya visits Sonya in her apartment. He sees her and is shocked by her appearance; Sonya looks so thin and impoverished. He questions how she has landed in such a state, and as he goes on to describe her depressing future, Sonya replies with naive simplicity, "God will not allow it to be so." Rodya, however, realizes there are only three options available to her, and all of them are hopeless. It is a heavy tale, bringing up dark themes that matched our current situation all too closely.

Oh, why on earth did I choose this book to read aloud?

Without warning, Yura suddenly broke down into inconsolable tears. He cried and cried as I held him gently, helpless to take away his hurt. The moment is imprinted on my soul, and I will never forget the sorrow of this sixteen-year-old boy who needed his mother so desperately. Yura had a bond with Mama that neither Zarina nor I had shared, but we stayed with him in his grief until he fell asleep on the floor. We never spoke about that evening and Yura's great pain—we simply didn't know how.

◆ ◆ ◆

LATER THAT WEEK, ZARINA DECIDED TO GO AND LIVE IN MAMA'S OLD apartment with her son. She still held me accountable for not being there to help her when Mama was so sick.

"It would have been better if you'd sent money to us instead of buying your air ticket," she told me. "You're the eldest and you should be looking after your family. This is not enough, Marina, and I'm going back."

There was too much pain between us to navigate. No one had any idea how hard it had been for me to gather enough funds to leave Norway, and I was blamed for not doing enough. I also believed the blame to be mine, and for many years I continued to believe this lie.

CHAPTER EIGHTEEN

ZARINA LIVED IN MAMA'S OLD APARTMENT FOR SOME TIME BEFORE selling it unexpectedly. In her naivety, she did so without speaking to Yura or myself. She thought she could buy another apartment and still have money left over, but she spent part of the funds from the sale on new clothes and partying. Then the rest of the money was stolen from her, and once again she had nowhere to live. Years later, we talked about losing our mother's home, and I know Zarina regretted her decision then. Now, we are both more understanding about how hard it was for Zarina to make good choices, particularly due to the lack of guidance or wise decisions we'd experienced in our family.

Yura stayed with me in the studio apartment. To him, it was normal to lie and steal—this was how he was used to dealing with his troubles, and now he used these tactics to try to help me too. But I also fell back into my old way of solving problems. One day, I came home to find my brother naked with a girl. Anger exploded from deep within me. I beat them both severely, breaking two of Yura's ribs.

Yura left after that. We did not know how to manage conflict with each other, nor did we know how to express our emotions and reason with one another or even explain how we felt. As a result, any one of us could unpredictably explode with rage. My brother and I have come a long way since then, and now we can even laugh about it. But at the time, the consequences were devastating—broken relationships, crushing pain, and self-medication—to name a few.

Alone and racked with guilt and pain, I kept drinking and stopped going to church—it was no longer a place of hope or answers for me. I still knew that God was my Papa and that he deeply loved me, but I had shut down so completely that I no longer knew how to feel his love.

I see now that, in the midst of this dark time, he kept looking after me in the gentlest and most patient way. He believed in me then and he believes in me now, and I know he always will. His love is truly unconditional—my life is a testimony to this. Only his unconditional love could heal the trauma in our family and change the tragic course of our lives.

But back then, I was hopelessly trapped in a downward spiral of slow and relentless self-destruction, self-medicating through alcohol and shutting myself away from everyone. I knew I needed to get out of the country or I would not make it, but that would not be happening for a while. I was trapped, drowning in deep sadness and lost in a minefield of shattered hopes. My only prayer was one of sheer desperation: "God . . . hold on to me!"

◆ ◆ ◆

I STAYED IN THE STUDIO APARTMENT AND KEPT WORKING AT THE INTERnet café, and Yura moved back in with me. As I walked to work each day, I noticed a 'working girl' who often staked out a certain spot on the street, just near the entrance to a public park. I smiled at her each day as I passed, and after a week or so she began to smile back. Sometimes I stopped walking to chat with her for a few minutes, which often meant men approaching me also to ask, "How much?" In the past, I would have lashed out at them, but something was happening in my heart, and now I simply sent them on their way. I had no energy for anger, only sorrow.

Over a period of time, I gradually gained my new friend's trust, and eventually, she invited me back to her 'den'. Her home was nothing more than a run-down, filthy apartment where drug-addicted prostitutes gathered to get high. I watched as the girls re-used old needles and tried to find a place to inject various substances into their bruised arms, legs and even stomachs. Most of them had run out of untouched places where they could inject themselves, and my heart ached for them and their hopelessness. I sat with them as they welcomed the numbing effect of the drugs. There was not much I could do other than be present.

"Would you like to come and live with me?" I asked my friend one day, and to my surprise, she agreed. She had only been with me for a week when she began experiencing heavy withdrawal symptoms. I had to work, meaning I could not stay with her all the time to watch over her, and soon she left to go back to the filthy hovel. The pain from withdrawals was too much for her to bear, and she gave up my quiet and safe home to chase after that high. Incredibly, she never stole from me, despite most drug addicts seeking any opportunity to fund their addiction.

I went back to visiting with my friend on the street, but one day I arrived to see her usual spot was empty. I went to her den to look for her, but no one knew where she was. I never saw her again. For the longest time, whenever I went past that park, I searched for a glimpse of her, hoping I might see her back at her post. But in my heart, I knew she was gone. I also knew that it could just as easily have been me.

CHAPTER NINETEEN

ALWAYS LOOKING FOR MORE WORK SO THAT I COULD SUPPORT Zarina, David and Yura, I was quick to follow up on a tip from Rano, a friend from my old church in Khujand. Rano mentioned a woman and her daughter who had developed a promising business and were looking for help, and I eagerly agreed to meet Valya and her daughter Tanya.

On arrival at their apartment, the door was opened by Valya, a lovely-looking woman in her early sixties. "Come in, Marina. Welcome. Rano has told us lots of good things about you."

Mother and daughter were friendly and outgoing, and their apartment was tidy and bright. I immediately felt comfortable in their presence, and we easily fell into friendly conversation. Unfortunately, they informed me that, although there was no work at present, there was likely to be some coming up later. But it was not a wasted trip, as I found myself striking up a friendship with Tanya, the daughter, who was in her thirties. I loved her company; she was so different from anyone I'd grown up with. Generous and kind towards me, I soon began to consider Tanya a good friend. She had a car and she often took me with her to her tennis practice. Then we'd go back to the apartment where we'd talk and laugh, enjoying the wonderful food that Valya prepared. I hung out at their place a lot, soaking in their easy friendship and warmth.

One day after my shift at the café had ended, I made my way to their apartment to be greeted by a business proposition from Tanya. It sounded so appealing, I immediately accepted. I didn't understand anything about the business deals she was involved in, but I trusted her to guide me as a friend.

"I'll go with you," she said generously. "These are the papers you'll be taking into the businesses we visit, but you'll need to sign them yourself when you're there. Once all the deals have been signed and confirmed, we'll send you to Russia all expenses paid, plus we'll pay you a wage, and you'll remain there for six months."

"What do you think?" she asked with a smile.

I could send money back to Zarina and Yura when I'm in Russia, I reasoned with myself. *It sounds easy ... but I feel a bit uncomfortable. Why?*

But I ignored my discomfort and set off with Tanya. Over the next few days, we traveled to various parts of Khujand city, visiting a range of businesses. At each new place, I met the owner and then signed some forms. *I'm feeling a bit uneasy,* I noted to myself as I signed yet another stack of invoices and receipts in a shabby office at the rear of a factory. Tanya was clearly avoiding giving me any explanation as to what was going on, and the more papers I signed, the more uneasy I felt. But Tanya kept assuring me that everything was fine.

Some weeks into my new job, Rano came to speak to me. At first I was confused when she asked me if I understood what Valya and Tanya were doing in their business, but it turned out she was just as helplessly tangled as I was in what was turning out to be a dangerous mess of illegal activity.

As I listened with a sinking heart, Rano explained that Tanya and Valya had found a questionable loophole in the tax law and were shamelessly exploiting it. Setting up fake companies in someone else's name, they were carrying out countless illegal transactions without paying any taxes.

Probably feeling guilty for involving me in their scheme, Rano had finally decided to come clean, brokenly telling me of her sister, Inna, who had been used by Tanya and Valya the same way I was currently being used. As it was Inna's signature on the legal papers for these fake companies, she was therefore deemed responsible for all financial transactions that took place while she was far away in Russia, 'waiting it out' before she was to return, six months later. What she did not know was that she could never come back to Tajikistan as there was now a warrant out for her arrest, and she owed thousands of dollars to the tax department.

Valya and Tanya, on the other hand, had emerged from the situation clean and with no proof of their involvement because Inna had signed everything. Tanya had then told Rano that if she could find another person for them to exploit, they would help to clear Inna's name so she could return home to Tajikistan. This was, of course, a lie, but she had not known it at the time when, desperate to free her sister, he had connected me with the duo.

I was broken-hearted to hear the truth. Life was already so tough for me and my family, and now I was suffering the pain and very real consequences of Valya and Tanya's betrayal. I had no idea what to do, as I was already so deeply involved. Unless I left the country before everything came out into the open, I faced prison. But if I left, I would be unable to ever return—just like Inna—when the tax department finally caught up to the papers I had so unwittingly signed. In the end, I decided to have a chat with Tanya and tell her honestly about my situation, without letting her realize that I knew the truth. Perhaps she would listen and respond with compassion to my story.

◆ ◆ ◆

I sipped my coffee as I sat with Valya and Tanya in their nice apartment. As we chatted, I shifted the conversation towards the personal, genuinely opening my heart and sharing about the painful death of my mother and how I was now struggling to look after my younger siblings and nephew. I was vulnerable and honest, and my tears were real. "I'm all the security they have," I said softly. "If anything happens to me, it leaves them without any support."

"Why do you think anything will happen to you, Marina?" Tanya asked.

Does she know how uncomfortable I am feeling about the job? I wondered.

Then, in response to her own question, Tanya gently reassured me as she'd done many times before that everything they were doing was legal and above board.

With that response, I knew without a doubt that these women were using me. They did not care about me or my family at all, and I decided then and there to go to the police. Presenting myself and exposing the operation would in itself be risky, due to the widespread corruption in my country, but I had no other option. I could not flee the country and leave my family behind, never to return.

As soon as I left Valya and Tanya's apartment, I walked straight to the police station. A detective listened to my story, then brought in an officer who specialized in working with tax fraud. I was in quite deep—they could see that—but their words were encouraging: "If you help us with this, we can arrange for some compensation to cover what you've lost."

The two police officers questioned me, consulting each other, and eventually came up with a plan that would hopefully provide solid evidence that I was being set up. They wanted to prove that I was being tricked into signing blank forms and being used in the cover-up for illegal tax evasion. The plan was risky and—for me—scary, but I agreed to do it.

The next morning, I arrived at Valya and Tanya's place ready for another day of business meetings. Tucked into my shirt was a hidden recording device, and the plan was for me to wear this throughout all my meetings that day with Tanya. I had been briefed by the police with some specific questions to ask that would help prove Tanya's illegal activities as well as verify the fact that I was being set up. My heart was beating fast, but I'd had considerable experience in hiding my emotions. As we went about our day, I carried out our conversations with outward calm and normality.

One of the places we visited was a rundown rug factory. In prior years it had been a flourishing business that made good quality, expensive

Persian rugs, but the business was no longer in production. Tanya came with me as I followed the owner into a dingy office at the rear of the factory, where I was asked to sign a stack of unnumbered and unnamed invoices and receipts. Leaving the office, I took several deep breaths to calm myself before heading back to the car where Tanya was preparing for our next appointment.

"Thanks, Marina," she absently said, flipping through papers. "Now we're going to pop into an importing company in this same street."

"Tanya, what are those unnamed forms for, and why did I have to sign them?"

Tanya shuffled the documents on her lap, distracted. "Mmmm, sorry, what did you say?"

"I just want to make sure I'm not violating any laws here. Can you explain again to me what those forms are for?"

"Oh, we're just going to sell some rugs, but we need a signature to show that the items are legitimately coming from the company," she replied. And with that, she unknowingly gave herself up, proving her guilt with no room for doubt.

◆ ◆ ◆

Tanya and Valya, both 'middle people' in the transactions, were arrested on charges of tax fraud, with me being the number one witness at the trial.

As I nervously waited to enter the courtroom, Tanya came across me in the foyer, and there she unleashed a stream of vicious verbal abuse, threatening both me and my family with retribution. Fortunately, the police officers heard all of this, and by now I had gained favor with the detective and the tax fraud officer by aiding their investigation. They warned the pair not to come near me again, though Valya and Tanya were not held for long. The judge released the two women with nothing more than a solemn caution—a verdict directly related to their wealth and connections.

◆ ◆ ◆

As for me, I was free. It had been a narrow escape, but while I was grateful that the police had helped me out of this mess, they never gave me the promised compensation. Valya and Tanya gave no thought to the suffering of their victims, and Inna was left unable to return to Tajikistan, while I found myself financially broke. I was destitute, but at least I wasn't in prison. Still, I felt as though I was slipping away again into darker places. I began drinking to numb the pain, and no matter how hard I tried, I could not see a way forward in Tajikistan. It was my homeland, but I had no support network, no recognized qualifications—which are essential to get anywhere in this country—and no contacts to obtain a job that would offer wages decent enough to cover the basics of rent and food. My part-time internet café job barely paid enough to cover the rent, and I couldn't go on struggling for a simple meal, let alone trying to support my family.

I knew I would need to look beyond my own country again, so I began browsing my options while working at the internet café. Unlimited access to the internet and plenty of spare time on my shifts meant I had ample opportunity to search online for work in other countries. Soon I came across a website called *Great Au Pairs*. Perhaps I could find work there? And with that tiny sliver of hope, I uploaded a profile for myself, seeking a job in the United States.

CHAPTER TWENTY

I N MY IMAGINATION, I COULD ALREADY SEE THE STATUE OF LIBERTY before me. I was walking the streets of New York and experiencing American life. I could hear the traffic, marvel at the thousands of people rushing and laughing and talking, see the flower sellers serving their customers . . . I could even smell the hot dogs being sold at pop-up stands on every corner.

The sheer depths of my desperation to change our family's circumstances—to free us from our generational history of brokenness and poverty—gave me the impetus to make this drastic move. I'm often asked how I managed, not only to qualify for an American work visa from Tajikistan but also to obtain my full US citizenship. The answer is that it truly was a miracle. And it all began with my personal dream to walk the New York streets.

Not long after I'd posted my profile on *Great Au Pairs,* I was contacted by a family with four children and a baby on the way. We immediately stepped into a lovely connection, and I believe it was God's arrangement more than anything else, as the whole process of my getting to the United States was so miraculous in itself.

The family agreed to be my host family in America, and they kindly sponsored my visa application. Their contract with me even included paying for my air travel. My next step was to apply for a US visa using my Tajik passport, and I made the trip to our capital city, Dushanbe, to visit the US Embassy there.

Last in line and waiting for an interview with the consular officer, I passed the time chatting with the people ahead of me. Most of them were from Tajikistan, though there was a Russian couple just in front of me. They were obviously well-connected and had money to further assist their case. One man who'd already been sitting in the waiting room when I arrived, emerged from the consular interview room with a long face. *Probably not eligible for a visa,* I thought to myself, feeling a twinge of concern. I had no money or connections myself, so I was probably going to be denied too. I was only twenty-two, single, and with no higher education or any skills to speak of. Nor did I have any intention of returning to Tajikistan in the near future. Most often, all of these factors would be an automatic 'no' for the person applying for a US visa.

My turn came, and I steeled myself for disappointment. I opened the door to the interview room and was greeted by the smiling face of the embassy officer. After my interview, he left the room before returning with my Tajik passport. He handed it to me with another smile. "Welcome to the United States."

I was speechless. I could not believe it! I wanted to jump up and hug the man right then and there. This was unquestionably the favor of God.

Before I left for America, I made arrangements to send money to my brother and sister, via a local family who were hosting Yura while he finished his school years. Zarina and her little son David had found a place to live with friends.

Ready and excited to begin a new life as an au pair, I arrived in the United States via Newark Liberty Airport, just west of New York City. My visa required that I attend a week-long introduction course for entry into the country. Unfortunately, I had been so excited in the whirlwind of plans and preparations that I had missed reading some key instructions. I assumed someone would meet me at the airport, and I spent hours roaming around the huge international terminal before learning that I was to make my own way to the hotel where I'd be staying for that whole week.

But nothing could dampen my excitement, and I made my way to the accommodation in good spirits, deciding upon arrival that the hotel was great! My room was comfortable and very clean, but I was far too excited to get a full night's sleep—even after so much travel. I had a couple of days to myself before the course began, so the first thing I did in the early hours of that morning, was figure out how to travel into New York City. I only had fifty dollars which had to last me for the week, but I had long dreamed of walking along the streets of New York and I did not want to delay.

I spent some time learning the train system, and once I was in Manhattan I walked up and down one street only to make sure I did not get lost. I walked around in absolute awe at the buildings and the people. To me, everyone looked like a model. People from all over the world flowed around me, and the city was so vast and beautiful that I could not stop staring at it all in wonder.

Several men catcalled me, and I was surprised that anyone would pay attention to me—I'd never thought of myself as overly attractive. In Tajikistan, girls get unwanted attention all the time, and I hated it. It was common practice for boys to run past and grab at the girls' breasts, and more than once I had fought with those who harassed me so. But now I was in New York, and I was amazed, not angry, to find people noticing me with appreciation.

Stopping at a McDonald's, I spoke in English, asking for 'fried potatoes'. I had translated the order literally in my head, and it took some back-and-forth discussion with the staff to figure out what I wanted. When I pointed to the picture, the girl serving me laughed, "Oh! French fries!" *No thanks, I don't want any 'fried French',* I thought to myself. *I just want some good Tajik fried potatoes.* But my English wasn't yet good enough to figure out the nuances of the American translations.

After enjoying my salty snack of 'fried French', I stopped at an out-door stall to ask the woman managing it how I could get to the 'Statue of Freedom'. She was puzzled, so I spoke slowly for her New York ears in my Tajik-accented English: "The big green lady with a torch of fire in her hand." In trying to say 'torch', I pronounced it 'touch'—I had asked for the big green lady with a touch of fire in her hand! Fortunately, the woman helpfully guessed the rest.

"Ah . . . you mean our good ol' Lady Liberty!"

However, she informed me that the Statue of Liberty was too far away for me to get there on foot. I would have to use public transport, but I decided against it as I was still afraid I'd get lost on my first day.

On the morning of my third day in America, I began my induction course into the US. My instructor was very friendly and funny. He laughingly told me I was the last person they'd expected would qualify for a visa. In fact, of the ten people who had applied for a visa on that same day, I was the only successful applicant! No one had ever been accepted from Tajikistan before.

God's hand was clearly upon this all, and I went on to spend the next eight years living in the USA.

When I sailed past the Statue of Liberty later that week, all I wanted to do was climb the monument. It was a dream come true.

◆ ◆ ◆

IN THE MEANTIME, BACK IN TAJIKISTAN, ZARINA HAD LOST ALL HOPE. At just nineteen years of age, having sold Mama's apartment and losing all our money, she decided, like so many young and unskilled Tajik women, to go to Russia, where salaries were far better, to look for work.

Later, she told me the story . . .

"I couldn't afford my rent," she said. "I couldn't even afford food." With a broken heart, she decided to leave her young son in the care of another woman who also had a little boy, promising to send money for his care.

In Russia, Zarina was soon promised work with a family who needed a housekeeper and someone to look after the children. It seemed like the perfect offer—until she was taken to meet the family.

"Do you know why you're here?" the man asked her as she stood at the front door.

"Yes," Zarina replied politely, "I'm going to work as your housekeeper and look after your children."

To her great shock, the man replied, "You're going to look after me as well."

"What do you mean?" Zarina tried to ask, but she was quickly rebuked. "Silence!" the man said, "Go and get ready."

Suddenly realizing what was happening, Zarina grabbed a photo of me from her handbag and began to sob. Her mind was swirling.

Lord, why didn't I listen to my sister and leave together with her? Probably I would have been in a different place, and my life would be different.

"Who is this prostitute?" the man shouted, grabbing at my photo.

"She's my sister," Zarina wept, hoping to escape this awful situation. "I need to talk to her." But her pleas were in vain. The man abused her for hours.

Later that day, the pimp who had delivered Zarina turned up once more. "Come with me," he said. "We're taking you to the hospital to make sure you don't have any diseases."

"My family will find me," Zarina tried to threaten him, "and then there will be trouble."

Hearing her boldness, the man of the house turned on the pimp. "Why did you bring a smart one here?" he shouted. "I told you to bring a stupid village girl who doesn't understand anything! Not one who stands here claiming her rights!"

Mercifully, a kindly Russian man pieced together what was happening and managed to retrieve her passport. "Here's a train ticket to Tashkent," he said. Today, Zarina thanks God for the kindness of that man—and of a woman who saw her on the train and kindly took her to her home in Uzbekistan. "Have a shower and a rest," she said, "and then I'll call a taxi to get you back across the border and into Tajikistan."

Zarina arrived home in tears. She had expected to return from Russia with gifts and money to support her family, but here she was, back to begging and prostituting herself for money. It was hell on earth. How I wish I had known what was going on with her. If only I could have been there to rescue her and support her. *If only I could turn back time.*

CHAPTER TWENTY-ONE

BACK IN PENSACOLA, FLORIDA, MY AU PAIR FAMILY, WITH THEIR four children and a precious new baby, were friendly and fun to be with. For the first time in my life, I was living in a coastal area with lots of sunshine. The family bought me a bicycle so I could explore the flat, easy streets of Pensacola in my free time. I'd never owned a new bike, never mind a bike that was mine alone.

During that difficult year and a half in Tajikistan, before making the move to America, I hadn't been to church. I felt that my struggles were far too much for the people at my home church, and I couldn't relate to them. I still felt this way, and all my attempts to connect with God-loving people here in Pensacola felt distant and superficial.

One Saturday morning, browsing for churches online during my free time, I came across a Messianic Congregation. I didn't know what 'messianic congregation' meant, but their faith statement sounded beautiful and resonated with happy memories of the church I'd been a part of back home. Their website told me they held Saturday services, so I jumped straight on my bike and cycled for an hour to get there.

When I walked through the doors and into their space of worship at nine-thirty that morning, I instantly felt at home. The Messianic Congregation quickly became my community while I lived in Pensacola. I loved their liturgical style, and it was here that my love of the Bible really began and blossomed. I read books on Jewish culture, and this deeper insight opened my eyes to many things in the Bible that I had not understood before. The rabbi and his wife had invited me to their home for the Passover celebration, and it was a wonderful, enriching experience—it was also my first ever real Passover.

But their hospitality extended beyond celebrations and special events, as our rabbi and his wife opened their door to many young people who gathered at their house seeking fellowship. A few months after I'd arrived in Pensacola, on one such evening at the rabbi's open house, I met Jeff. At first we just enjoyed hanging out, but a deeper friendship and affection soon began to grow between us.

◆ ◆ ◆

"Jay, it's time to get off the computer now, you've had your time. Your mom says you're only allowed one hour today."

I was nervous laying down the law to ten-year-old Jay, as I'd had several difficult experiences of trying to fulfil the family's discipline protocols when neither parent was at home. Jay often defied me in his parents' absence, and this time he swore at me, completely refusing to comply.

"Come on, Jay, your mom told me to keep you to your time allowance on the computer."

"There's no way . . . I haven't finished this game. I'm just going to finish. Go away you . . ." He shouted at me rudely, his anger building.

I could feel my indignation mounting too, and that old, familiar sense of deep anger was rising in my gut. "Jay, get off that computer NOW!" My voice rang out, loud with authority. "I'll be telling your mom about this when she gets home." I was young and inexperienced, and I didn't know how to deal with this behaviour or how to communicate with an angry child.

Yelling further insults at me, he got up from the computer, grabbed the phone and his two younger siblings and slammed his bedroom door. I followed him angrily, but when I grabbed the door handle, it was locked. "I'm phoning the police!" he yelled. I could hear him still ranting on the other side of the door, "You wait 'til Mom gets home . . ."

Forced to wait until their mother arrived home, I couldn't say anything when she finally came through the front door. Instead, I emotionally shut down, fleeing the house and running barefoot out into the rain with tears streaming down my face. When I returned, feeling calmer but somewhat apprehensive, I found out that Jay lied to his parents about what had happened, and both parents had believed him. I was still not a very good communicator, and when someone pressed me or yelled at me, I inevitably shut down and went silent. As a result, I couldn't articulate clearly what had happened that afternoon.

The woman allocated by the au pair agency to support me and the family also happened to be a good friend of theirs. Fortunately, she saw both sides of the problem. She explained to the agency that it was a challenging situation for both parties, but that I was a good au pair.

The agency decided to relocate me on short notice, and they quickly found a six-month position on Hilton Head Island, on the coast of South Carolina. I moved immediately. Around this time, Jeff, who had finished his military service, left to return to his home in Kansas.

In contrast to the ups and downs of my Florida posting, the Hilton Head job was an amazing experience. I looked after two children—a three-year-old girl and a five-year-old boy—and had the time of my life. A Christian family, they were very kind and respectful towards me. The father even taught me how to drive. I also soaked in the beauty of Hilton Head Island, a gorgeous place interlaced with waterways and bordered on the east by beautiful, golden-sand beaches. I soon made a couple of friends from Europe, also au pairs, and we spent much of our free time together, enjoying the cafés and the beaches, and doing what I'd never been able to do before . . . just being a lively young woman and enjoying the simplicity, predictability, and security of life in a beautiful place. I loved being with this new family, but by the end of the first few months, I was struggling with how difficult it was to see Jeff, who now lived in Kansas, over one thousand miles away.

As my six-month commitment to the Hilton Head family drew to a close, I asked the agency to find me something closer to Kansas.

Accordingly, they offered me a position with a family in Sioux City, South Dakota, only a four-hour drive from Kansas.

◆ ◆ ◆

WORKING FOR THE LITTLE FAMILY IN SIOUX CITY WAS A JOY. I LOVED their three-month-old baby boy, and they welcomed Jeff coming to visit me there. Once a month he came to me, and once a month I made the eight-hour round-trip, traveling to visit him in Kansas. This arrangement meant we saw each other twice a month, and in between we spoke on the phone or messaged each other as much as we could. There wasn't a lot of opportunity for in-person communication, but we made our growing relationship work, even if it was long-distance.

◆ ◆ ◆

I'M GOING TO WRITE MY DENTAL APPOINTMENT ON THE FAMILY CALENDAR, I TOLD myself. *Then that'll give everyone plenty of notice.* As well as putting my appointment on their shared calendar, I made sure to tell the family that it was coming up soon. I'd waited some months to get this special appointment to fix a painful tooth, and I knew it wouldn't be easy to reschedule if I missed it.

On the day of my appointment, the home phone rang: "Marina, sorry, I'm not going to make it back in time. I've got a heap of work to finish today."

"But I told you about this in advance so I wouldn't have to miss it. I have . . . to . . . get to this appointment!" My agitation sounded through the phone, but there was no response. I missed my appointment, and I was left terribly upset by the family's indifference.

That evening, once everyone was home, I tried to explain my distress, reminding them again how important this appointment was and why I'd written it on the calendar. But the conversation didn't go well at all, and they ended up asking me to leave. To my horror, they informed the au pair agency that I'd been slamming doors and was unsafe to be around their son. I had no voice in the matter, and I wasn't asked to explain my side of the story.

I leaned on Jeff for support during this time, and he kindly offered me accommodation with his mother in Kansas, where he was still living. I gratefully accepted, and shortly after moving in, Jeff proposed to me. We were married in Kansas, one year after we'd first met at the Messianic Congregation in Pensacola, Florida.

YEARS LATER, AFTER I'D EVENTUALLY LEFT AMERICA, I CONTACTED THE mother of the family in Sioux City—the place I had been dismissed from after being reported as 'unsafe'. I assured her that I had loved her little boy, and I had been a good nanny to him, and she replied that she was now much more relaxed as a mom. I could understand her struggle back then being a first-time mother and having to work full-time. Nevertheless, it was another incident where my inability to express myself resulted in an unnecessarily broken relationship. I take responsibility now for my inadequate communication back then, as I can reflect on my past from a much better position.

CHAPTER TWENTY-TWO

As Jeff and I settled into married life in Kansas, I took on a volunteer job with Catholic Charities USA. I worked with refugees, and I loved what I did. Looking back, I can see God's favor was with me, as I was soon offered a full-time, paid position as a Refugee Case Worker. I later learned this was a much sought-after job.

Jeff and I began to enjoy life in Kansas. We bought a nice second-hand car, and I was now able to send some money back to my family in Tajikistan. I had a great team at work. Together we helped refugees transition into American life as smoothly as possible, aiming to empower them to become more independent. I found this job very rewarding. Soon I was advocating for refugees in all manner of civic and governmental interactions. I also helped them navigate the US immigration system to ensure their arrival and initial support plans were organized.

Just as I had been so graciously received and welcomed into the country, I now helped new arrivals adapt to the American culture, assisting them in searching for employment and securing medical services. I would help them create a budget and manage their finances. Our funding was minimal, but our team was highly effective. We genuinely cared about the people we were helping, and I experienced a sense of God's purpose for my life growing and stretching.

During this happy time, I applied for a course of study in criminal justice at the local community college. University study was a long-held dream of mine, and I felt that now was the time to pursue it. With studies added to a full-time job, my life became busy—very busy. Especially with the addition of a playful Akita-Husky puppy I named *Severa*.

But cracks were starting to appear in my relationship with Jeff. I had never spoken with him about my past or told him of the trauma

I'd experienced growing up. I came from a family who never shared anything of our experiences—especially if it was traumatic. In turn, Jeff did not share much with me either. We both had hurts from the past, but neither of us knew how to deal with those hurts or communicate our thoughts and needs to each other.

With so much of my time consumed by work and learning, I was eager to spend any spare time with Jeff. But that's all it was—Jeff was only able to access my spare time. He was not very happy with my high level of commitment to work and studies, and I began to feel alone and unsupported. *Why can't he understand?* He soon slipped into a routine of hanging out with a few old friends who loved weed and board games. Jeff and his friends could easily stay up the whole night playing games and smoking together. I had nothing in common with this group, and I didn't enjoy sharing my precious spare time with them.

Our married life began to slip into a never-ending roller coaster of emotional reactions as we raced through the motions of life together. We worked out together, we went on the odd date, we occasionally visited the Messianic Synagogue, but mostly we just sat and watched television in weary silence.

During this stressful season, I began experiencing severe pain under my shoulder blade. Eventually, it spread throughout my whole body. "You have fibromyalgia, Marina," the doctor told me. "I'm going to trial a new drug that may help you."

Over the next few months, he tried out various treatments but they only made me feel worse, and the pain got no better. Living with low-grade chronic pain affects your whole being—you live with an invisible disability, and as the pain gradually wears you down, it impacts not only your body but your emotions too.

◆ ◆ ◆

ONE EVENING, I SAT DOWN TO WORK ON A STUDY ASSIGNMENT. I WAS using Jeff's computer as mine was at work, and my eyes were drawn to 'recent searches'. *Hmm, shall I?*

I clicked, and his latest search popped up: "Why is my wife always angry?"

Does he see me like that?

It makes me so sad.

Why is this happening?

I was at a loss as to how to fix this downward spiral. Our relationship progressively deteriorated, and we constantly fought about lots of little things.

"I need the Ford—you take the old Honda," Jeff insisted.

"But I bought that car," I shot back. "And it's reliable for me."

"Too bad. I do a lot more driving than you."

Things continued to escalate, and late one night I found myself in such severe pain that I decided to take myself to the emergency department at the local hospital. Really, I wanted Jeff to take care of me, but he was playing a boardgame with three of his friends. I looked over at them laughing and having fun. I wanted Jeff to help me get to the hospital, but I didn't ask him—I couldn't. Several hours later, still in pain even after a morphine shot, I drove myself home.

Realizing we desperately needed help, we decided to go to counseling together. We learned about better ways to communicate with each other, but a month went by and there was no noticeable difference in our relationship. There seemed to be no hope, and eventually, we decided that I would move out and we would file for divorce later down the track.

We had been married for only three years.

◆ ◆ ◆

THERE WAS NO ONE AROUND FOR ME WHEN I HIT ROCK BOTTOM. I DIDN'T have any people that I felt safe to reach out to, as I had neglected my own social life while married to Jeff. Vulnerability is not my strongest trait, and though I knew a lot of people at work, they didn't know the extent of the turmoil currently buffeting my personal life. They'd heard about my health challenges and my divorce and were very understanding when I took some time off—but that was it. I could not share with anyone what was really happening.

Not only was I dealing with emotional and physical pain, I was now also in financial trouble. I had not been attentive to my own financial situation whilst married—for example, I'd neglected to put my name on the ownership papers of the Ford vehicle I had bought. When I left Jeff's house, instead of taking the Ford which I had paid for, I found myself leaving with the old Honda which we had never properly maintained.

Unsurprisingly, I was soon involved in a serious accident when the Honda's brakes suddenly failed. The vehicle was written off, and I was left badly shaken. I phoned Jeff for help—after all, he was still my husband—but his response was not what I'd expected: "You left the house; I don't have to take care of you."

Why would I expect anything different? Jeff had never 'taken care' of me anyway. I had worked fulltime, but when I enrolled in studies, he had guided me to take out a big student loan which helped him to pay off his own debt, as my student loan attracted a much lower interest rate. In my ignorance, I had also allowed him to complete all my income tax forms which he did incorrectly, leaving me with an IRD debt as well. I had trusted Jeff with all of my finances, not questioning any of his suggestions at the time, but now my situation had become a painful lesson for me.

Consumed with his own pain, none of my problems seemed to register in Jeff's mind. His family blamed me for hurting their boy, and I felt the brunt of their anger in their harsh treatment towards me. I no longer had a family. I had no one who could advocate on my behalf, and

I was in no fit state to advocate for myself. Grateful that I still had my job, I silently dealt with the daily and debilitating physical pain, on top of all my worries. I only had one friend who I could speak with honestly.

The emotional pain of our marriage falling apart and the physical pain of fibromyalgia were such an intense combination that I began entertaining thoughts of suicide. In the face of overwhelming challenges, I was returning to my old default thought processes. *I'm in so much pain. How can I carry on?* Thankfully, God seemed very close through those difficult times. Brokenness indeed kept me in a cycle of destruction, but it was his nearness that kept me from spiralling into complete despair.

One afternoon, as I found myself making yet another suicide plan, the Holy Spirit prompted me with a very clear thought that what I was suffering from was a chemical imbalance in my brain. Perhaps if there had been a community of believers around me, I may never have got so trapped in those cycles. Thankfully, however, I had one friend I could turn to.

"What's the matter, Marina?" she asked. My whole body shook from the tension of heavily suppressed despair as I began confiding my thoughts.

"I just cannot think straight or even look with any hope at my future," I sobbed.

Seeing the state I was in, my friend's husband took me to the emergency department of the hospital, where I was immediately admitted to the mental health ward. The psychiatrist who attended me prescribed medication and registered me for group therapy sessions. I refused everything offered: "No—I don't want medication, and I'm not going to group sessions to listen to everyone else's tragedies on top of my own!"

I just want love and support! I screamed silently. Still, I remained in the hospital and slept for several days. When I left the hospital, I realized God was the only one who could help me. *I'm never going to do this again,* I decided. The only thing left to do was to cry out to God.

◆ ◆ ◆

As soon as my divorce from Jeff officially came through, I became aware of a new threat—losing my US visa, which was dependent on my marriage status.

Pain and hardship draw out the best and worst in us, I thought miserably to myself. It certainly worked that way for me. As my mind became clear and the pain of this fresh grief began to recede, I pondered on how certain people come into our lives and make their mark on us, as many had on me. There were people in my life whose presence had revealed a hidden darkness in my heart, and there were people whose presence had highlighted the gold I did not know was within me.

Finding the capacity to forgive Jeff and his family became my new focus, as I allowed God to gently touch my pain. I spent hours crying, but I knew I wasn't alone. My heart tiptoed around my part in the destruction of our marriage, and I became aware of the effect my brokenness had had on my relationship with Jeff. There were life skills I had never learned, and I could see that now.

As I faced the sorrow and the revelations it brought, God immersed me in the warm depths of his loving comfort while I mourned. I rested, and a tiny green shoot of hope began to spring up within me.

CHAPTER TWENTY-THREE

O R *HaOlam*, THE MESSIANIC CONGREGATION THAT JEFF AND I HAD occasionally attended, welcomed me back with love and acceptance. I noticed that I was no longer holding people at a distance. I felt safe and enfolded in the loving care of these friends, and I knew I would flourish again. I was also surrounded by wonderful people in my workplace. The friendships I was building both in my work with *Catholic Charities USA* and among the *Or HaOlam* congregation were authentic and deep, and they carried me through a very difficult time in my life. Care and support were poured out on me, and I grew and matured emotionally and spiritually. I am forever grateful.

My US visa was still under threat because of my divorce, and I dreaded having to sort this out. In practical ways, *Or HaOlam* helped me prove that my marriage had been real, and not one organized for the sake of immigration status. Again, God's help was with me.

◆ ◆ ◆

AS I LOOKED OUT OVER THE LARGE NUMBER OF FELLOW APPLICANTS AT the United States Naturalization Ceremony, I marvelled at our numbers. There were over two thousand of us, and here I was, not applying for a visa extension but receiving my *full* US citizenship.

"Marina Kurban. Tajikistan."

The host called out my name and country, and I jumped to my feet. A huge cheer rose from the audience as I filed up to the stage to collect my Certificate of Citizenship. Half the *Or HaOlam* congregation attended the event, celebrating with me in great joy.

◆ ◆ ◆

ON YOM KIPPUR—THE DAY OF ATONEMENT IN THE JEWISH CALENDAR—something extraordinary happened. The congregation had gathered to fast and pray together for our own forgiveness and for generational transgressions. As we recited the deep, heartfelt prayers, I felt as though a warm and heavy blanket was being draped over me. Comfort. Comfort. Comfort. I began to weep until my sobbing intensified so much I had to leave the main room.

In a classroom downstairs, I knelt on the floor alone. I could barely hold up the weight of the holy presence upon me. Comfort, comfort, comfort—God's presence was engulfing me, and I wept for what felt like hours. As I knelt, I sensed my heavenly Papa telling me to rise and place my hand on the world map which hung on the wall of the classroom. With a great deal of effort, I pulled myself up off the floor and made my way to the map, placing my hand on it as waves and waves of tears continued to flood me. I had no idea what was happening or even what I was praying. When the tears finally began subsiding, I opened my eyes and let my hand fall from the map. It was then that, absolutely shocked, I noticed my hand had been resting directly over the country of my birth: *Tajikistan.* In that same moment, I heard God speak clearly into my mind:

"Will you partner with me and become a conduit for my healing into the land and people you have tried to run from?"

I didn't need time to consider.

"*YES!*" I responded.

In awe, I realized that, for the first time, I felt a profound love swelling within me for my land and my people. The fierce anger I had held towards those who abused women and children had fled away. The lurking darkness, built up over years of anger and resentment, had miraculously been replaced with compassion, empathy, love, and a longing to help.

God himself had stepped into all the gaps of my life, filling in the spaces of all that I'd missed out on growing up simply because my mama didn't have the capacity to provide everything I needed. There were layers of emotional, physical, spiritual, and mental neglect, and I had missed so many normal developmental milestones as a result. And yet, gratitude now flooded my heart.

Gratitude to the One who had filled my heart with his love, who had prepared me by placing people in my life who loved me well, and who had softened and healed my broken heart, completely changing my world view. It was a true and complete transformation, and I joyfully confirmed my *yes*.

WHEN I LOOK BACK AND CONSIDER THE PERPETRATORS OF ALL THE abuse towards my grandmother, my mama, my sister, and my friends—and yes, myself too—I understand so much more than I did back then. I used to see the person committing the abuse as a heartless, worthless human being. I felt so much disgust and anger towards them, and I wanted to see justice done. I didn't see the broken child trapped within the adult body.

Later, as I came to know God's love for me, I realized that those who had abused my mama, my sister, and my friends, are as much victims as those they abused. They were all in need of someone to love them and believe in them. These men had once been little boys who were neglected and abused themselves. They had no adults in their lives to model honor, kindness, or love. I knew these kinds of boys. I grew up with some of them. Recently, I was struck by something I read by US author and teacher, Suzanne Arms:

> "If we hope to create a non-violent world where respect and
> kindness replace fear and hatred, we must begin with how
> we treat each other at the beginning of life. For that is where

our deepest patterns are set. From these roots grow fear and alienation—or love and trust."[2]

Though I didn't know it at the time, my *yes* to God was founded on this insight—long before I recognized these words as the underpinning of the vision I would come to live by.

---

2   Arms, S. (2012, May 15). Birthing The Future.

CHAPTER TWENTY-FOUR

THREE YEARS AFTER MY DIVORCE BECAME OFFICIAL—AND EIGHT months after my Yom Kippur 'transformation'—I began planning another visit to Tajikistan. I wanted to love and serve my family, and I wanted to understand better how to pursue the vision God had given me in that classroom.

Happy and content in my current job as a nanny for another wonderful family, I was able to easily book a break, during which I began to organize my trip. My preparations were split between two main focuses: funding and family.

Sourcing the funds for an air ticket home would require a miracle. I had no assets, and I was living from my paycheck without being able to save anything on the side.

I also felt nervous about returning home. Ensuring that I was emotionally and spiritually secure for this visit would require some help. My history of being short-tempered, as well as our dysfunctional family relationships, had been a problem on previous trips, and I hoped I was mature enough to handle this visit.

My whole life, I had felt the pressure of responsibility for my brother's and sister's pain, and the aftermath of their bad decisions. This burden was something I was still working through, and I had a few sessions with a counselor to help me prepare for any probable challenging moments—I didn't want to react in my old, familiar patterns.

I planned to be away for a month, with the focus of my trip mainly being my family. Friends in the United States helped me gather gifts to take home, and I decided on practical things like water filters, nutritional supplements, warm clothing, and some US dollars to spend on my nephews. My awareness of and gratitude for God's help was heightened when my employers, Jess and Margaret, asked to speak to me after a day of gift shopping.

"Marina, we'd like to pay for your return air ticket—and no refusing our gift!"

They had begun to understand what was starting to form in my heart for my people and my country, and they found joy in assisting this journey.

◆ ◆ ◆

BACK IN TAJIKISTAN, I WAS DELIGHTED TO BE REUNITED WITH MY SISTER Zarina, my brother Yura, and my two nephews, ten-year-old David and five-year-old Danis. It had been eight long years since I'd been home, and I hoped we could create some good memories together. Every day I made time to have fun with my nephews.

"Do you want to go to the park and play on the swings?" I asked David and Danis. "Let's get some *lepeshka* on the way."

"YES!" they shouted, jumping around and dragging me out the door. We all loved the special Tajik naan bread—the most beautiful of the flat breads, it was shaped into circles and stamped with different designs around the edge according to who had made them. They were pieces of edible art.

I decided to use the small amount of money I had to take Yura to the dentist. All his teeth were in terrible condition, and some of them were severely misaligned. The dentist removed some of his teeth and spent a lot of time giving the rest a good clean. It was a very painful and unpleasant experience for him.

Even though I was spending plenty of quality time with my family, pouring out all my gifts and covering all our expenses, I still noticed the tension between us. I grieved our broken childhood. We had not spent much time just playing as children—being brother and sisters growing up together.

Zarina and Yura still argued a lot, and I found myself caught between the two, trying to be the peacemaker. However, the lying and manipulation they used on each other was too much for me to bear, and even when this was not happening, they still managed to push all my emotional buttons. Eventually, I had to leave the house and stay with one of my friends to take a break from it all.

Despite the counseling sessions I'd had before my visit, I felt defeated—as though I had hardly changed. Here I was, still reacting to difficult family situations by becoming angry and resentful. I felt extreme guilt over not being able to properly cover Zarina's needs for her family. She was depending on me for this, and I was afraid that she would resort to prostitution again as a way of providing for her children, just as our mother had done.

Unfortunately, nobody in my family could grasp how difficult life was for me financially. Because I was living and working in the United States, they assumed I had money to spare and US dollars falling out of my pockets. Being the oldest meant there was an expectation that I would cover the needs of my younger siblings.

Zarina often asked me for money, but she would not be completely honest about how she spent anything that I gave her for living expenses.

"I know you need more, Zarina, but I can't give you more!"

"How can you do this to us?" she retorted angrily.

I now know that the desperation of survival does this—it makes lying and manipulation the norm. Survival mode says that in order for me to survive, you need to give me more—I don't even consider how hard life might be for you.

By the end of my stay, I found myself coming to terms with the situation. I had done the best I could during my month-long visit, and I figured, *It is what it is.* I still wished for so much more for my family. Zarina and I weren't able to connect and just be sisters. Our scars were still creating unhealthy habits and relational dysfunction that would take much, much more time to heal. I was leaving Tajikistan still longing for a proper chance to strengthen our relationships together, but I wanted to at least leave my homeland on good terms with my family.

CHAPTER TWENTY-FIVE

EMPTY-HANDED AND EMPTY-HEARTED, I RETURNED TO KANSAS with no clear vision of my future. All I knew was that I didn't want to live a paycheck-to-paycheck existence for the rest of my life. There had to be something more. I had hoped God would direct my steps with some sort of obvious sign, such as a bolt of lightning, but I saw nothing to show me how I could serve my homeland and my people. My visit to Tajikistan had left me feeling inadequate, as I realized I couldn't even hold things together for my own family.

How can I equip and empower people and show them what is possible with God? How can I be a channel of his love and resources?

The questions rattled around my head in despair.

How can I fulfil this dream when I don't even know what the dream looks like?

Hidden within me, silent and barely breathing, the dream slept.

ALTHOUGH I FELT NO SENSE OF DIRECTION AT ALL, I EXPERIENCED GOD'S love in action yet again when I became more deeply involved with the *Or HaOlam* congregation in Kansas. I discovered how much I enjoyed working in groups with others, and I became involved in the leadership of the worship and creative outreach teams. Not only was this fun, it was a great opportunity to grow closer in my friendships and to work through my old impulse to keep a sense of 'distance'.

As I adjusted to life after my marriage, God's love gently nurtured me. The congregation became my family, and I experienced a genuine connection and a deep sense of belonging with them. It was a wonderful time of growth, and I cherish those memories.

After my divorce from Jeff, I decided I didn't want to be alone anymore. I decided to try an online Christian dating site where I met a man from New Zealand. We connected well, and soon we were spending hours and hours chatting online and enjoying great conversations with each other. After a few months, he came to visit me in Kansas, and we seemed to be a good match.

"I really want you to come and see New Zealand, Marina," he told me eagerly. "You can stay in Auckland— it's the biggest city in the country, and much bigger than Kansas City! We could also take some time to explore the South Island and see the southern mountains."

Having lived for some years now in the flat landscape of Kansas, I wanted to experience mountains again. The rugged mountains and glacier-fed streams that cover most of Tajikistan were often in my memories, and I missed the sight of majestic peaks rising into the sky. We agreed that the next step would be for me to visit him in his home city of Auckland, and I began to prepare for another overseas journey.

I spent four months with Jeff in Auckland, and by that time I could see that we should end our relationship. Our mountain visit never happened, and I returned to Kansas. However, it wasn't our final goodbye, as we continued to spend a lot of time talking online. We were honest with each other, but our relationship was an unsettled emotional roller coaster—just like our marriage had been. We both clearly still had wounds that needed healing, and we were both looking for safety and stability in each other.

"I'm coming back to see you," I asserted confidently after a year and a half of ongoing conversation. "Maybe we can work things out properly in person."

That Christmas, two years after my first trip, I made preparations to travel to New Zealand again. Full of hope, this time I decided to make a new start. I resigned from my job, resigned from my leadership roles at *Or HaOlam* and said a last goodbye to all my friends.

◆ ◆ ◆

COMING IN TO LAND AT AUCKLAND AIRPORT, I WAS CAPTIVATED BY THE sparkling turquoise waters that played around the islands of the harbor. Tree-lined bays and long stretches of golden-sand beaches shone in the early morning light. I sensed a welcome emanating from this land, but I didn't know why. Nor did I understand that my gaping wounds still needed much time to heal.

Settling in Auckland was easy. I quickly found a job as a caregiver for the elderly, and a kind, older couple offered me a place to live, charging a very reasonable rent.

I thought about where my life was going and pondered the man I had met. *Now we can get to know each other in person. We'll have plenty of time to spend together, and we can talk and enjoy life.*

But we could no longer keep the parts of us hidden that we had covered up when we spoke at a distance. *How could I have been so blind?* Three months later, I ended our relationship completely.

It was a painful but healthy decision, yet here I was again—alone and without much money, stuck in a small country in the far south of the Pacific Ocean. My decision to come to New Zealand now felt like a huge diversion. My only option was to return to the US, find another job and keep doing what I had been doing—living from paycheck to paycheck, struggling to support my family back home in Tajikistan. *I am such a failure,* I wept to myself. I had no one to care about me or help me, and I began questioning all of my life decisions. My thoughts were turning back on me, and I saw the edges of my old patterns begin to curl around, ready to entrap me in despair once again.

No! an insistent voice deep within me shouted out. *There's no way I'm going back to ordinary life again.*

I had no peace about returning to Kansas, and I knew I had to pursue the dream that was still burning inside me. There was so much more to my life. I could sense that truth, even if I didn't know how to make it a reality.

Should I? Can I? How?

In the end, I let everything go and took a hefty risk.

I used my American credit card to pay for a bus ticket to the very south of the South Island of New Zealand—the place where the snowy mountains touch the sky. *Te Waipounamu* (pronounced Teh-why-pour-nah-moo in the Māori language) is a place of water and greenstone, and the beauty of God's creativity, and I was about to find out what—if anything—it would reveal to me.

CHAPTER TWENTY-SIX

THE STRONG CALL OF THE MOUNTAINS IS WHAT DREW ME SOUTH. I had heard of the Southern Alps, the magnificent mountain range running along the spine of the South Island—and I wanted to see this area before I left New Zealand for good.

I'm always in my element when surrounded by mountains and water. Khujand, my hometown, is only an hour's walk from the mountains, and the foothills of the famous Pamir and Alay Mountains were my childhood playground. It was only when I left Tajikistan that I realized how beautiful my homeland is—and that mountains are a big part of the reason.

Traveling slowly by bus to one of the southernmost towns in New Zealand, I eventually reached the small, rural town of Gore. I knew no one and had very little money, and I was rapidly accumulating credit card debt as I continued to try and provide for my family back in Tajikistan.

Step by step, the first door slowly opened to me. In the small local store, I got talking to a woman from a farming family. She offered me board and food if I would come and help her with the children and do some odd jobs around the farm for about a month. The family was incredibly kind to me, and when my month was up, they referred me to another farming family in the area who needed a nanny. Here I earned my board as well as a small wage that covered the support I sent to Zarina. I had no money left over for myself.

Despite my gratitude, this was a challenging time—it seemed like nothing was happening in my life. I was living in the middle of nowhere at the southernmost end of the Southern Alps of New Zealand, where the most exciting things in life are trout fishing, hunting, and bringing the sheep in for shearing. I had no idea where to go next or what to do with my life.

Nothing seemed to be happening, but strangely, at the same time, incredible things *did* happen during my nine months on this farm. I had more free time on my hands than I had ever had in my life. I read, wrote, and took long walks, talking to God as I explored the farm and the surrounding forests. It was such a restful and enriching experience—something I didn't even know I needed. My intimacy with God was deepening, and he began to take me further into his aching heart for his beloved humanity.

One evening, as I was listening to my Papa in my heart, a song came into my mind. God was singing to me about his daughters—the ones caught up in human trafficking and sexual exploitation. I thought about what he had said to me in that classroom back in Kansas, when his cloak of love and comfort had rested on me with such weight.

As I listened, Papa began showing me his broken heart for the world and his longing for the restoration of humanity.

Can I go where you go, Lord?

I was ready to go back to Tajikistan if that was on his heart.

"*When I go—will you come with me?*" I sang. "*How many times I have prayed, Lord 'Break my heart for what breaks yours.' And now I feel the pain, I need to go, I need to bring your daughters home. I can see what you see. I can feel what you feel; I hear their cries. I'm going to bring your daughters home.*"

He spoke again. "Take my hand and I will teach you how to fly. Hold my hand and I will teach you . . ."

More and more songs followed as a flood of ideas and pictures poured into my mind. Maybe I would apply for nursing training at the university two hours away from here. If I could study nursing, I could become financially self-sufficient. Then I could return to Tajikistan and follow God's plan.

More pictures and words streamed rapidly into my mind's eye.

I could see a healing centre, a home, and many similar centres located all around the world.

Shalom Homes, I thought, remembering the lavish abundance in that word 'shalom'.

Oh yes, these places will be homes of healing, restoration, development, and empowerment for individuals and families affected by the devastating realities of poverty, abuse and human trafficking. They will be places that people can call home. Places where people will be family—experiencing love that runs deep. They will experience the sort of safety which leads to freedom, and find a new future. And that's what will create hope.

My heart was full. I was picturing individuals and families growing to become leaders who would themselves influence others for positive change in their own nations.

Little did I know then that God was going to bring these dreams into reality very quickly—in fact, within the next few years. However, before any of this happened, he was still working in me. I found myself adjusting my heart to hear from him in ways that were much more expressive than I'd experienced before. I had given God permission to speak to me in any creative way he wanted, and now I was saying to him, *I will listen.*

"May I pay for your lunch?" she asked.

And as we sat and ate together, chatting about what had brought each of us to this conference, I told her some of my story.

Janet Hutchison's act of kindness in buying me lunch at a Christian conference was the catalyst that encouraged me to look deeper into the significance of my journey and the potential stories I had within me to share. Up until this point, I had never shared anything about my upbringing with anyone. It was all still too painful for me, and I did not see much value in digging up the past. Besides, I wasn't practiced at it—in my own family, sharing our stories was just not something we did. In fact, in our Tajik culture, we usually hid our stories if they were bad.

But Janet's next question was about to change all of that.

"Would you come and tell your story at our church?"

Janet and her husband, Edward, who both became very much a part of my life, were pastors of a small church near Gore, the town where I was currently living and working on the farm.

I hesitated, realizing I'd never spoken to anyone about my life before.

"Thank you for asking me," I replied. "Can I think about this, and I'll catch up with you before the end of the weekend?"

On the final evening of the conference, a Māori pastor called Norm MacLeod was speaking about the dramatic and effective ministry in their church towards gang members and prostitutes.

That's where I belong, I thought. *That's what I want to do—help them, love them, serve them.*

When the service was over, I was gathering my things from under my chair when I was surprised to see Norm himself approaching me.

"There's a greatness about you, and God wants me to impart to you what he's given me to carry," he said quietly.

A 'greatness'? I had no idea what he was talking about.

Norm called a couple of other church leaders over to join us, and he asked me if they could all pray for me.

"Yes," I answered, remembering my agreement with Papa to listen to his creative ways of leading me.

Being lifted up in prayer by this group was amazing—powerful. I felt an awakening shift in my spirit. One of the men prayed, "This is a time of acceleration; what would have taken ten years will be done in half the time."

None of these people knew anything about me or my dreams for the future, yet each word they spoke resonated within me—even while I couldn't fully understand what was happening.

Eventually, the final day came to a close, and I went to find Janet.

"Yes, I'll come and speak," I told her.

◆ ◆ ◆

How do I tell people my life story? What do I say?

I thought about the encounter that had saved me from taking my own life when I was fourteen, and I cried and cried. I spent hours on the farm, just writing and crying. For the first time ever, I wrote down my story. The writing revived bad memories from my childhood. I remembered the constant, unresolved stress of living in survival. I grieved the loss of my younger years and the fact I'd never had a loving sibling relationship with my brother and sister.

My heart ached for Yura. Even today, he says he is not ready to share his story. He feels his past is too dark, and that his life is not yet a testimony. I know it is, as I have walked with him all these years. The very fact that he is alive is an absolute miracle. There have been so many times that he was on a brink of death and God miraculously came through for him. Despite the hell on earth that he has been through, Yura loves God and has managed to keep his heart soft. He still dreams of opening a home for children, especially children with disabilities, as they are amongst the most marginalised in Tajikistan. I hope that one day he will be able to tell his story as a reflection of the deep love that the Father has for him, but as I began writing, I realized his story is not mine to share.

My heart ached also for the loss of Mama, and for the brokenness and pain of Zarina and so many of my friends. As I wrote, I was looking back . . . but I was also reaching forward, firmly clasping the hand of him who is Hope.

◆ ◆ ◆

On a bright Sunday morning, I stood in a little church in a tiny farming town in southern New Zealand, facing an expectant audience. I shared my story for the first time, and as I did so I realized I was speaking not only out of pain but also out of healing.

I had been broken by anger and hate, but now I spoke from the powerful, restoring love of God—how only he could have transformed my pain into blessing as I loved him amid my darkest difficulties.

The fact that I could stand before an unknown audience and speak my journey and heart was evidence enough that something most remarkable was happening.

CHAPTER TWENTY-SEVEN

S I FINISHED MY STORY, I REALIZED THAT THE WORDS HAD BEEN tumbling from my mouth as easily as water flows downhill. The people in this church had heard the miracles God had performed. They had heard my pain, but they had also heard my hope. And through it all, Papa saturated me with all the love I didn't have and all the needs that hadn't been met—all the things I'd missed out on since I was a little child.

Edward stepped forward to close the service, handing me an envelope—a 'koha' (pronounced *kaw-ha*, meaning a gift or a donation from the heart). Immediately, I felt Holy Spirit whisper to me, "Give it back. Don't even open the envelope. Give it all back to the church."

I didn't hesitate, I gave it all back as a gift from the heart of God to this beautiful church.

Later, as I left the building, I called out to Edward and Janet, "I'll walk back to your house. See you there."

I began to walk along the country road, and it wasn't long before I heard a vehicle coming towards me. A new, very shiny farm truck pulled over, and a man rolled down his window to greet me.

"Hey, Marina!" he said excitedly. I was surprised but also pleased to see him, as I knew this man and his family. He jumped out of his truck, talking rapidly.

"My wife and I know about your situation. We prayed separately and both came up with the same sum, and now we'd like to give it to you."

I was speechless—I had just given back the *koha* the church had given me. It was also amazing that this man, who didn't live in the local area, happened to be driving along this very road as I walked to Janet and Edward's house. I was becoming much more practiced at hearing

Holy Spirit and taking action straight away, and I gladly accepted their gift. What this man and his wife didn't know was that it was exactly what I needed to be able to stay in New Zealand and take the next step.

◆ ◆ ◆

THE BIGGEST PROBLEM I HAD BEEN FACING WAS THAT MY VISITOR VISA for New Zealand was about to expire. I had discussed my dilemma with a respected counselor-friend, hoping for some advice.

"I hardly have any savings," I told him, "nowhere to live, and no family here. I'm not sure what to do. I couldn't bear to go back to the States. Life would just be about survival again."

He listened carefully. "Well, Marina, your circumstances suggest that the sensible decision would be to return to the States. But ask God about it first."

Should I stay in New Zealand? "God," I prayed. "*Please tell me if staying here will draw me closer to the dream, or will it simply be another distraction?*"

Logic stated I needed to go back to the United States and find a job, but my heart resisted. In the end, I decided to take the risk and stay in New Zealand.

But many practical things needed to be worked out. I needed a visa, for one. I had been told to apply for a 'religious worker' visa—meaning I could work within a religious organization—but this required supporting myself. However, I only had two hundred dollars in savings plus a credit card debt, and more importantly, no offer of a job in a religious organization.

But then I remembered that at the same Christian conference where I'd met the encouraging Māori pastor, Norm McLeod, I had also listened to a man named Benji Alexander. He had spoken about the work being done to make a film about slavery and the sex trade in Thailand, and it felt like familiar territory for me.

Benji had heard a little about my background while he was at the conference and had invited me to speak at his church in the deep south of New Zealand. And so I reached out to Benji. "Come!" he said. "I'll arrange for you to speak."

Making my way across the stunning South Island of New Zealand, my spirit began to soar. *The mountains. The clear skies. The long stretches of unspoiled road.* It reminded me of home, wherever that might be.

◆ ◆ ◆

THE NEXT FEW DAYS CHANGED THE TRAJECTORY OF MY LIFE. AFTER I spoke, Benji approached me with another invitation. "You speak Russian, don't you, Marina? Would you come with us to Thailand? It would be just Jodi our cameraman, you, and myself. We're going to connect with some Russian-speaking women who are trapped in the sex industry there, and you're the ideal person to come and help."

My heart was burning to be involved where there was the greatest need, and I quickly said, "Yes."

I had already decided to say *yes* whenever I knew God was leading me, and this 'burning in my heart' told me he was reassuring me to take this step.

Benji paid for all the expenses of the trip. It was my first visit to Thailand, and I fell in love with the country and the people. But as we strolled along some of the notorious streets of Bangkok and Pattaya cities, we witnessed the horror of the sex trade on a massive scale, including with very young children.

Heading past the Thai Go-Go bars in Pattaya City, we went into a Russian club. It was strange to be speaking my mother tongue again after years of English, but there were girls here from all over the former Soviet Union. It was obvious to those inside that we weren't customers—we just wanted to speak to some of the girls—and the atmosphere was tense. We were outsiders who were not to be trusted. After a while, we met Amina, a 'working girl' from Uzbekistan. We 'hired' her, and she came back with us to our hotel. We made it clear we did not need anything from her—we just wanted to chat. She was very apprehensive, telling us, "We—the girls and the pimps—are very cautious. The club where most of the Uzbek girls work was raided last week. We don't know who you are."

When we explained what we were doing, Amina nodded, but she still spoke cautiously. "I'm from Tashkent in Uzbekistan. I have two children. I've left them with my friend and I send her money every month to care for them." My heart sank. I knew this story all too well—it was what Zarina and so many of my friends had done. Even my mama had given herself for us.

Amina was here in Thailand willingly. She was young, uneducated and desperate to provide support for her family back home. "That's all," she finished abruptly. There was more to her story, but she was afraid we were recording her, even though we assured her we weren't. We paid her for her time, and she allowed us to pray for her before she left.

Late that same evening, Benji, Jodi and I walked along one of the streets to film some night-time city scenes. We stopped at a 7-Eleven— one of the many chain convenience stores. I waited outside, leaning against the wall while the two guys went inside to buy us something to eat. Movement under a streetlight caught my attention, and I looked across the street to see a massage parlour opposite. A tall Caucasian man with long hair was holding the arm of a little Asian boy. *Not much more than a toddler,* I estimated. *He must be only two or three years old. But something's not right—why is this toddler up so late? It's nearly midnight.*

A quick search on the internet will soon give you an idea of what massage parlours are used for in Pattaya. The man and the boy disappeared out of the streetlight and into the parlor, while I stood frozen in shock. In my heart, I knew what was happening. I wanted to scream. I wanted to run into the parlour and rescue the boy out of that man's hands, but I couldn't move.

By then, I was familiar enough with the law of the land to know that I could not do much anyway without photographic evidence of abuse. I desperately wanted to rationalize what I was seeing—perhaps the man worked there, and the boy was his son. Or maybe the little boy was the son of one of the working girls, and the man was looking after him. I went on and on thinking up reasonable explanations, but I knew the truth—I was witnessing the real depravity and misery of our world. Worse, I knew this was the reality for many children in Thailand and across the globe.

◆ ◆ ◆

I DID NOT SPEAK MUCH FOR THE REST OF THE NIGHT. I WAS SILENCED by what I had seen, and by the memories it had raised from my own childhood. Walking through the darkened streets with Benji and Jodi, I sensed the desperate cries for help echoing all around me.

As a child, all I had wanted was a safe home, enough food to eat, and to be an innocent kid and play with my friends without being afraid of being beaten or sexually abused. I'd wanted someone to rescue us, to help us, to make everything alright.

Now, my arms longed to open wide to every boy and girl on that darkened street—I wanted to hug and hold each one of them. The weight I felt was so enormous, I could barely stand. I looked around and saw children who had grown up too fast, children who would never have a chance to experience the innocence and playfulness of childhood. I could easily have been one of them, but I was now safely out and on the other side. How could I just leave them to suffer their fate? But also, what should I do about the growing desire within me to remain in New Zealand? Thankfully, I wasn't left in a quandary for long. "When we get back to New Zealand," Benji said, "Why don't you come and study with us at the Bible school in Te Anau?"[3]

The timing seemed right for me. My job on the farm near Gore had ended, and I had not managed to meet the requirements for entry

---

3 Pronounced Teh An-oe

into nursing training, due to my academic qualifications from Tajikistan and the US being insufficient. As a non-New Zealand citizen and an international student, it would cost me thousands of dollars to pay for my nursing studies. I also had a credit card debt to pay back.

Now, having received a generous gift from the man who had stopped me on the road, I found myself able to apply for a 'religious worker' visa after all. Still, I wanted to be sure. "Lord Jesus," I prayed. "Please show me what to do. Is this the next step or not?"

That very night, I had a dream. In the dream, Benji was standing in front of me with an open book and a gigantic smile on his face. Crystal-clear water flowed all around him, and I sensed such an atmosphere of peace and joy. I woke up knowing that I would move to Te Anau and join the Revival School team. All I needed now was a formal letter of invitation from the local church in Te Anau.

Within a very short space of time, my religious worker's visa was granted. It was nothing short of a miracle. From there, everything came together. Within a couple of months, I had been offered a place to live in Te Anau rent-free, and people in the Te Anau church ensured my Bible school fees for the next two years were covered. Not only was there enough money coming in to cover my basic expenses, there was even a little left over to send back home to Zarina. What an incredible moment it was when, just two years later, I was able to pay off my credit card debt in full and finally close my account.

CHAPTER TWENTY-EIGHT

I RELISHED EVERY PART OF MY STUDIES AT REVIVAL SCHOOL IN NEW Zealand. After my experience as a bible college student in Russia, I could hardly believe that adventure, games and fun were part of a Bible school curriculum. Learning about our glorious position as sons and daughters of the King, and how we are made to flourish and reign in the Kingdom of God, filled me with delight. But it was the joy of life and the fun we had that helped me most. Without even realizing it, I was beginning to trust God's heart for me more and more.

My first evening at Revival School was spent off-site in a forest. We pitched our tents, then followed the leaders through the forest, some distance from the camp. The evergreen beech trees with their small leaves created a dark and delicate canopy over us as the stars came out.

"Come on everybody," our leader called out, "Get into groups of ten." We followed Benji's lead. "Now I'm going to tie you all together," he explained, "either by your wrist or by your ankle, and we're going to navigate our way back to camp through the forest in the dark. This game is called, *The Burma Trail.*"

With only one compass and one flashlight between us, and our limbs tied to the person before and after, this was no easy task. For the next few hours, our ability to work as a team was being tested, and I found myself loving every minute of it!

Fun adventures like this were often part of our week, and they helped break me out of my older sister 'seriousness syndrome' as I called it—a persona formed from years of carrying too much responsibility on my shoulders as a child. The fun and interesting environment created by the leaders as part of the daily program was drawing out the best in me.

As we learned that we reflect God's kingdom everywhere we go, that we are essentially 'cultural architects', I began to understand my desire to make every place I find myself in feel like home and a place where people could thrive. I began to ask myself, *What does Love look like in this situation?* We discussed signs, wonders, miracles and acts of extravagant love as being windows that reveal heaven, and I was beginning to look through some of those windows.

◆ ◆ ◆

MISSION TRIPS WERE PART OF THE YEARLY CURRICULUM, AND I DECIDED my focus would be exploring opportunities to help others trapped in the same type of upbringing I'd been stuck in. It was during my last year of Bible school when I returned to Tajikistan once again—and it was in my hometown of Khujand that I reconnected with a project manager in the church I'd attended during my youth. He was delighted to see me. "Come to dinner, Marina, and we can catch up."

I had known this man and his family since I was sixteen years old. They were Russians with a deep love for the land of Tajikistan and its people.

"Now, tell me, what are you doing back in Tajikistan?" he asked as I shared a meal with his family.

"I have a dream to build a healing centre," I told them. "One right here in Tajikistan that uses a holistic approach. I want it to be a place where women and children who have survived human trafficking can come to be cared for and restored. One day, I'd like to build these centres all over the world. I want to equip, enable, and resource people who have been through some of the things I've experienced so they can heal and grow and become catalysts for positive change."

He paused to mull over my vision, then responded, ". . . Ah, well, there's a property here in Khujand that would be ideal."

I didn't tell him that, despite having lived in the United States and now New Zealand, I was not wealthy. I had no personal savings, and

I had spent the entirety of what I did have on this trip. Nevertheless, I decided to go with him to see the property.

It was a sweltering hot summer's day when we set out, and we arrived covered in sweat and dust. I was even less impressed by the property, which consisted of a windowless, unfinished brick building situated on a small block of barren soil. There was no shade in sight, and not even a blade of grass to be seen. I didn't feel encouraged at all.

No, this is not even close to the dream, I thought. But, as I stood sweating in the merciless heat, something shifted in my heart. I started seeing possibilities. It was like a veil was lifted away from my eyes and I could see clearly. I knew then that, even if it wasn't about this property, and despite having no tangible resources at all, I would still say *yes* to my Papa.

The cost of the property was far beyond what I could even 'dream' about. All I had were two hundred US dollars in cash and a ticket back to New Zealand. I wondered where in the world I would get the money to undertake such a vision. And finance was not the only obstacle. In Muslim countries—and many countries of the world—not-for-profit organizations are very closely monitored for religious activities.

Nevertheless, I left the place that day having quietly said *yes* to God. I knew he was inviting me to partner with him to make a difference, but I needed more clarity. I needed confirmation that this was not just one of my 'good ideas'. The vision I was carrying would require a miracle; my strength and determination alone would not be enough to pull this off.

THE NEXT MORNING, AS I HELD MY BIBLE, I ALLOWED IT TO OPEN TO A random page. I would not normally expect to hear from God in this way, but today I was looking everywhere I could for an answer. I looked down, and as I read the second chapter of Haggai, God spoke to me with clarity as I read. Five key points seemed to stand out as *his* strategy.

But it wasn't a strategy list of things I'd have to do—all I had to do was trust him and partner with him—it was a list of what *he* was going to do.

The first strategic promise was in verse four. "Be strong and work . . . for I am with you" (v. 4). Papa was saying to me, "Do what I have equipped you to do and leave the rest to me." This was about partnership!

Then I kept reading. "My Spirit remains among you. Do not fear" (v. 5). I knew that the Hebrew word for fear included a subtle secondary meaning, *'be strengthened'.*

"Do not fear, be strengthened, you and all people," God was saying to me. I held on to the substance of those verses and found my spirit uplifted.

The next thing God showed me was that he would shake off any man-made plans, opinions or traditional beliefs that had corrupted the land and the identity of its people. Turning back to the passage, I read the words: "In a little while I will shake the heavens and the earth, the sea, and the dry land. I will shake the nations" (v. 6).

This was exciting! God was letting me know he would infiltrate my homeland with his culture—the kingdom culture that reveals our true human identity. I could sense his longing to partner with what we were doing.

I began reading the following verses. "What is desired by all nations will come, and I will fill this house with glory. The silver is mine and the gold is mine" (v. 7-8).

I began to see that he had already started to make provisions and that this would come 'from the nations'. My job now was to work in partnership with him, communicating to others how they could be a part of loving the world in this practical way.

Finally, I lingered on verse nine: "In this place I will grant peace." For a few moments, I reflected on the Hebrew word for 'shalom'. Shalom is more than just the English definition of peace. It is a powerful state that shatters chaos and darkness. Papa's promise to me was that everything would function according to his divine design!

As I read over the passage, I realized that God meant it all literally. I began weeping with joy as I said *yes* again, and my tears quickly turned to excitement as I grasped the idea that I would have a real part in the unfolding of God's beautiful love within my native land.

◆ ◆ ◆

ON MY RETURN TO NEW ZEALAND, I WAS ASKED TO SPEAK AT A LITTLE church in the south of the country. As I shared the story of my life and my dream, I felt that I should also tell them about what had happened while I was in Khujand. In the end, as my speaking drew to a close, I briefly mentioned Papa's strategy from Haggai chapter two. I read the whole chapter, ending with the verse that mentions all nations uniting for the purpose of love:

> *"What is desired by all nations will come, and I will fill*
> *this house with glory. The silver is mine and the gold is*
> *mine," declares the Lord Almighty.*
> *Haggai 2:7-8*

I beamed at the people before me who were listening intently.

"This is what he has promised," I said with visible joy. "That he will bring the provision from the nations themselves."

A few weeks later, I received a phone call.

"Hey, Marina, my wife and I heard you speak at our church, and we'd like to come and see you."

"Yes, of course. I'm home this afternoon."

Later that day, I sat down with this man and his wife in my home. I offered them tea, and we enjoyed laughing and talking together as we watched their children play. When it came time for them to leave, the husband placed a box on the table. His wife looked on with a smile as he spoke for both of them:

"When you were reading that verse from Haggai, God spoke clearly to us. He said, 'You have silver and gold—will you give it?'"

He gently pushed the box over to me.

"This is for the vision God has given you, Marina."

I reached out to take the box, finding it surprisingly heavy. I opened it slowly, not knowing what to expect, and stared in awe at the contents.

Never in my life had I seen real silver or real gold bullion. But nestled inside that box were ten one-kilogram bars of silver and six one-ounce gold bullion coins.

I was sure I heard Papa God laughing in delight.

EPILOGUE

AT THE AGE OF FOURTEEN, AND ON THE VERGE OF DESTRUCTION, someone reached out to me. Someone heard the cry of my spirit and said *yes* to my desperate plea. I decided then and there that I would say *yes* every step of the way, even though I had no idea of how or when. Viewing my own experience with some objectivity when I visited Thailand gave me a huge understanding about how to help others who were trapped as I had been. I was touched by my Papa's compassionate heart.

My upbringing in a brothel in Tajikistan had not given me any awareness of a loving God. Despite that, the 'someone' who found me at fourteen was my heavenly Papa. Now that I know him personally, my life is intertwined with his gentle leading. He's given me all I need for life in all its richness. I've experienced the miraculous, I've experienced provision, and suddenly, 'the dream' is possible.

In my youth, life was one big struggle. I was an angry child living in survival mode, trying to protect my brother and sister and even pull my mama out of the despair we all lived in. I marvel that as I cried out for help and began dreaming of a loving family, God placed me in two amazing foster families, which changed the trajectory of my life. I have no doubt that what saved me from self-destruction were the many people along the way who loved me deeply and believed in me.

An implicit trust in the goodness of my heavenly Papa has since developed in me. I even have the joy of my own family now. One evening, when I went into the play hut to call my children for dinner, I found my husband, exhausted, lying on the floor. Our little girl had painted his back, face, hair, legs, and arms in glorious colors. And in response, we laughed and laughed. I am so grateful that God empowered me with his love, **honor** and gentleness—this has completely broken the cycle of generational dysfunction in my family.

Being a parent is one of the most wonderful and challenging things I've ever done, and I love it because I have such an amazing Papa. If any of our children ever make a bad decision or choose a self-destructive behaviour, I never want them to feel, *I can't go to Mom.* I don't ever want them to feel ashamed. In fact, I want the opposite. I hope they will run to me for support—because that's the type of parent I have in Papa. He has this amazing ability to make me feel so safe and secure, regardless of the decisions that I've made—and I've made some stupid decisions that have caused me great pain. Yet I still run to him. I will always run to him because of how safe I feel with him. He never pretends with me. He has never made me feel guilty or ashamed, or that I'm a less lovable person because of my mistakes. It's quite the opposite—the bigger the fall, the more of his love and patience I feel.

As a child, I never thought my dreams and longings for the future could work out. But now it's different—remarkable even with the way my Papa calls me into dreaming with him. I never think, *Oh, I really don't want to do that,* or only do something because I want to serve God. Instead, I think, *Whoa, I get to do this with my Creator?!* He invites me into partnership with him, and it's as if he's saying, "I think so highly of you, I love you so much and I trust you." Then I feel like I'm the child being crowned—the royal son or daughter becoming the next king or queen. He is still speaking to me in so many different ways—in dreams and longings, in circumstances, and as I read my Bible. He is always growing my sensitivity towards him.

When I felt my Papa's presence all around me and within me, I was a little girl without a father, without a loving mother. Just a child who picked up a book and saw Jesus with children surrounding him and climbing onto his knee. That picture planted a seed in my heart, and it sent me on a lifelong journey. I had no idea where I was going, and now he's brought me here.

My childhood yearning to protect my brother and sister, and to help Mama provide for us, turned me into an angry activist wanting to force change. I was always an adventurer seeking more, daring to go to other places and take risks. Now I've learned that I was made like that—God put everything in me right from the very beginning of my life. The difference is that now I can see how he's empowered me with his love and helped me to grasp his life within me. He's given me all I need for life—all the skills to partner with him in his big vision.

The Spirit of the Lord God is on me, because the Lord has anointed me to bring good news to the poor. He has sent me to heal the brokenhearted, to proclaim liberty to the captives and freedom to the prisoners.
Isaiah 61:1 CSB

На мне Дух Божий! Меня выбрал Господь, чтобы всех бедняков обрадовать, а также утешить всех, кто опечален. Меня послал Он сказать всем пленным, что они свободны, всем узникам, что их освободили.
ИСАИЯ 61:1 ERV-RU

My dear reader,
I would like to pray a blessing over you, just as I bless my
children every day.

*You are a gift from heaven to this world—a delight and
deeply loved. I bless you in the name of Jesus. I bless your
spirit, your soul, your body, and your mind.*

*May God's perfect Shalom rest upon you, and may his
favor be with you in all your comings and goings.*

*May your joy remain constant, and may your light shine
brightly all the days of your life. I bless all the generations
before you and those yet to come.*

May you see your children's children.

*May you walk with your Creator in the garden of
your heart, love him as he loves you, and know
him as he knows you.*

May it be so.

ABOUT 'INVEST IN A LIFE'

By now, you've read my story. You know the challenging upbringing my brother, sister and I survived, along with many of our friends and other neighborhood children. Every person in my immediate family has been affected in some way by the harrowing realities of poverty, abuse, and commercial sexual exploitation and trafficking. Sadly, most of those family members and close friends were touched by these atrocities at a very young age.

Back then, there were no welfare agencies for people to turn to for help, and unfortunately, this remains the case for many vulnerable and impoverished communities in Asia even today. Most who have tried to escape their status and live a normal life simply can't manage it due to the lack of resources, skills and support.

For as long as I can remember, my dream has been to change this reality. On a small scale, I have been able to make an impact by providing resources to enable my family and other individuals to escape the traps of poverty, abuse and enslavement. In Tajikistan, our first *House of Shalom* is nearly completed, funded by the silver and gold and other financial gifts we have so generously been given.

But in recent years, I have begun to believe that God has an even greater vision than mine. I see *Houses of Shalom* spread throughout Central Asia and beyond, centres of healing, restoration, development and empowerment for individuals and families affected by the devastating realities of abuse and human trafficking. In these houses, everyone is family, experiencing a genuine love that runs deep, a safety that creates freedom, and a new future that creates hope. I see homes where individuals and families can dream again, and where those who were once beaten down can be newly empowered and equipped—and ultimately become leaders and catalysts themselves of the positive change we seek, not only for our nation, but around the world.

To find out more about *Invest in a Life*, please visit:
www.investinalife.org

Watch more of Marina's story on her YouTube channel:
@MarinaKurban2586

A BACKGROUND OF TAJIKISTAN

I WAS BORN IN TAJIKISTAN (OR *TOJIKISTON* IN THE NATIVE TAJIK LAN-guage); a landlocked country situated at the end of the Himalayan Mountain chain, and the smallest nation in Central Asia. It is smaller than the South Island of New Zealand or the U.S. state of Wisconsin— about half the size of Italy. The capital and largest city is Dushanbe, situated east of the Varzob River which runs right down the middle of the country.

More than ninety percent of Tajikistan's land is mountainous, and these mountains are magnificent. Part of the area of Central Asia known as 'The Roof of the World', Tajikistan's landscape is dominated by the Pamir and Alay ranges, with its highest peak, Qullai Ismoili Somoni, soaring to almost 24,590 feet (7,495 meters).

2025 statistics state that Tajikistan has a population of 10.8 million people, with eighty-five percent identifying as Sunni Muslims. The spoken languages are Tajik, the official language, Uzbek, the language of neighboring Uzbekistan, and Russian. Whilst Russian is widely spoken in government and business, three-quarters of the country is rural and speaks mostly Tajik.

Tajikistan has a long history in trade, due to its location along the famous 'Silk Road'. The ancient roots of the country are Persian, but around a thousand years after the birth of Christ, the country was swallowed up by war and occupied by the Ottoman Turkic Empire which also encompassed neighboring Kazakhstan, Kyrgyzstan, and Turkmenistan.

From the mid-1800s, the Russian Empire took control of the Tajik territories. Russia's influence and its associated repression only increased over the years, despite growing resistance and attempts to gain independence.

The American Civil War in the early 1860s interrupted the worldwide supply of cotton fiber, so Russia turned to Central Asia as an alternative site for cotton-growing. The substitution of cotton for food crops in Tajikistan created no major problem initially—until the Russian Revolution in 1917 led to Tajikistan being completely cut off from Russian-sourced grain supplies. Local farmers turned back to growing grain instead of cotton, but previous military actions taken by the anti-Communist groups had already destroyed many of the rural irrigation systems. This lack of reliable irrigation resulted in yet another drop in grain production and further unrest.

At the end of 1917, Vladimir Lenin announced a policy to eliminate the *kulaks*—the land-owning Russian peasants who were wealthy enough to own animals and employ labour to work on their farms. Land, property and resources were immediately confiscated from the *kulaks* and redistributed without any compensation for those original farm owners.

Joseph Stalin followed up Lenin's pronouncement with an order for the 'liquidation of the *kulaks* as a class', and this became a foundational part of his social engineering policies. By the end of January 1930, all *kulaks* were either shot or imprisoned, as decided by the local secret police. Many were sent to Siberia or Kazakhstan to work in hard labour camps, while others, evicted from their own properties, were used in labour colonies within their own districts.

As wealthy *kulaks* in Crimea, my great-grandparents were among those forced off their land and executed like so many others. In the ensuing chaos, the family was torn apart, and my grandmother, Alla, ended up in an orphanage, having lost all connection with her family. Her father and brothers were sent to fight the Germans, and as far as I know, there are no further records of them.

As a fully-fledged member of the Soviet Union, Tajikistan underwent a drastic social and economic transformation. Dams were constructed for electric power generation and irrigation, and industry was rapidly developed. The village formerly known as Stalinabad became Dushanbe—a modern capital city. However, despite all these changes, Tajikistan remained the poorest republic within the Soviet Union.

Following the collapse of the USSR (Union of Soviet Socialist Republics) in 1990, Tajikistan declared its independence from Russia. More Tajiks were becoming politically active, but the new leadership did not have the capability to lead a brand-new country—particularly one that was poor, impatient for change, and with more than half the population aged under sixteen. Existing undercurrents of political and social turmoil degenerated into protest, and soon the unrest turned into civil war.

Communists fought to retain power in the face of an opposing alliance of Islamic and democratic forces, and the war moved across southern Tajikistan. During this time, both Communist and Islamic militias looted and burned their way through much of the southern farmlands, driving thousands of families from their homes into the capital of Dushanbe or into the mountains. More than a million people were displaced in and around the country.

A treaty was signed in 1991, ending the civil war, and numerous villages were rebuilt. Once again, there was a growing sense of community and determination to rise from the ruin. Families returned to live next door to other families who had been bitter enemies during the Civil War. Cheptura, one of the new villages built near Dushanbe, is where my parents, Galina and Rustam went to live when they were first married.

While the peace talks made allowance for a democratic process and opposing political parties, Tajikistan has had only three changes of government since 1991, as the presidential term is seven years. It remains the poorest country in Central Asia, with thirty-five percent of the population falling below the poverty line. The last elections in 2020 made little progress to the country's status, and the criminal and political violence remains a great obstacle to Tajikistan's ability to engage internationally and reach a place of nationwide prosperity and peace.

A LETTER FROM MY MOTHER

HELLO, MY DARLING, I LOVE YOU DEARLY AND LONG TO SEE YOU. I WORRY about you and pray that everything will work out for you. May all your dreams come true. I love you deeply and think about you day and night. Even though Zarina and you didn't tell me, I found out that Zarina is two months pregnant. I tried hard to keep my emotions in check; it is unfortunate, but somehow we will survive this as well.

Yura is still attending school. He loves and misses you and always asks when you will be back. As for me, I am living as I always have—someone needs to pay the bills. Although my legs betray me and my liver is acting up as well, that is okay. The most important thing is that all of you turn out to be decent, intelligent, and healthy human beings, my darlings. You need to help me a bit, as I will not last forever.

We have received your letter and photos. It looks like you have gotten thinner. You haven't told me that life is hard for you, but I will pray for you, my darling, that you will always have hope for victory and in your dreams. Thank you for your help, but please do not send any more money—I am managing. I am looking for work and hope to move to Kairokum, closer to the lake. Do not let your spirit down.

P.S. Please send me your address. I want to return your money. Take care of yourself. It is my deepest desire that you will be alright.

(Note from Marina: The whole letter was a surprise, as Mom did not normally talk to me this way. It was gentle, and I could feel the love. There was also a little note from Yura which broke my heart. It mentioned me taking them away from Tajikistan. That was always a dream for all of us that one day I would be able to get them out of Tajikistan.)

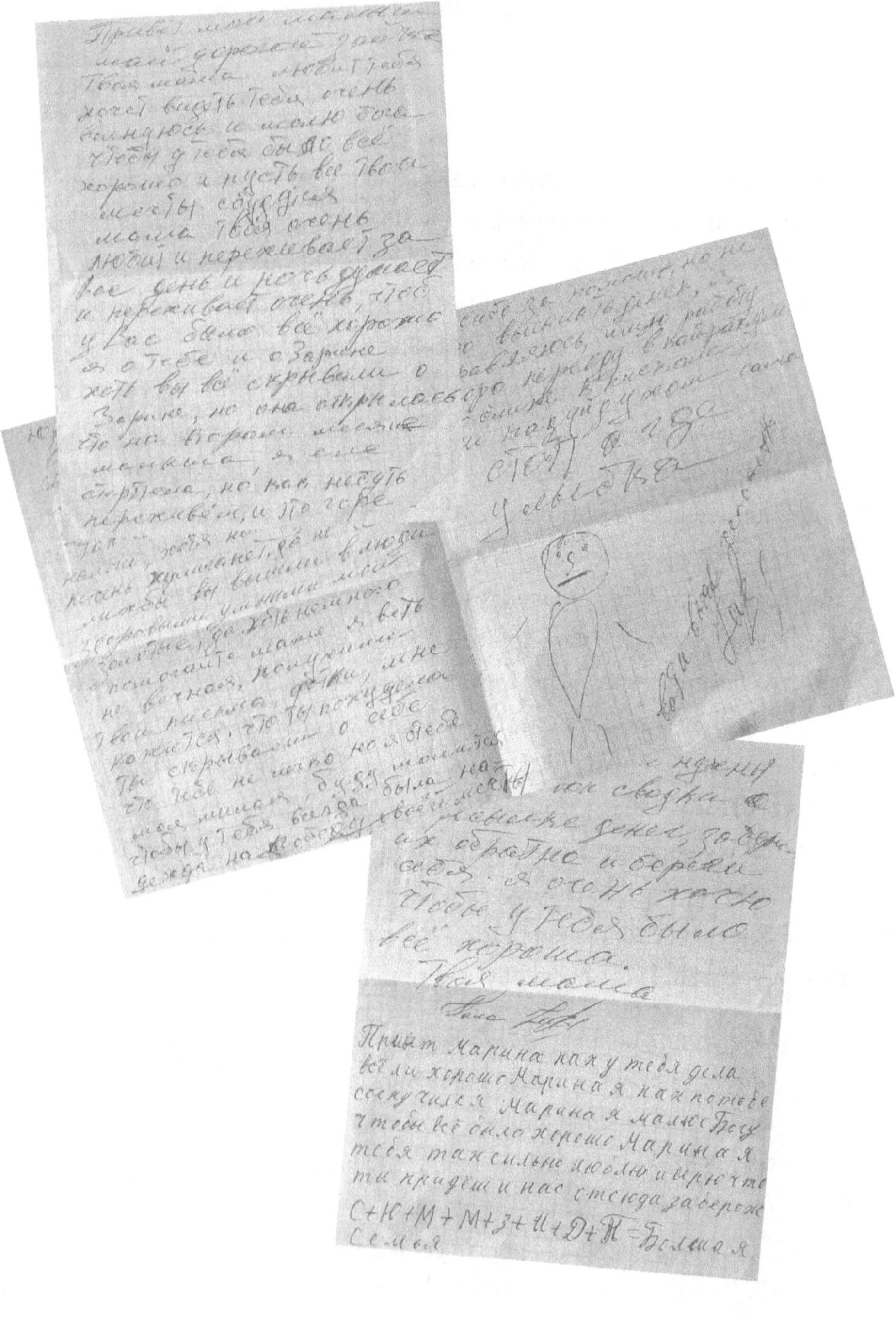

PHOTO GALLERY

Dad, Mom and Angelica

Mom and I

Zarina and I

Mom

My Parents and I

157

My Grandmother
and I

Mum and Yura during
my visit from Norway

Marina and Ryan
with Eliakim
and Sogdiana

ACKNOWLEDGMENTS

To my Maker. Thank you for your unconditional love and unwavering guidance.

To my husband, Ryan. I am deeply grateful to call you my best friend. You are an incredible husband and father, exceeding every dream I could have had.

To my children, Sogdiana and Eliakim. Being your *mamochka* (Mommy) is my greatest privilege and joy. You have shown me a depth of love I never knew I had. You are truly a kiss of grace from heaven.

To my Mom. I believe I chose you when God sent me to this earth, and I wouldn't change a thing. Thank you for being my anchor.

To my siblings, Zarina and Yura. Loving you gave me the strength to carry on when I thought I had none left. I am deeply grateful for you.

To my dear nephews, David and Danis. May you come to know and experience the profound depth of love that unconditionally flows from your Creator. In that love, you will find the essence of life itself and the freedom to truly live.

To my foster parents, Rune and Kari Borgso, and Arthur and Larisa Musayelyan. Thank you for saying yes. Your relentless love and belief in me have shaped the woman I am today.

To the team at Torn Curtain Publishing, and especially Anya McKee and Penelope Dawson. You took my scattered thoughts and turned them into a novel that I couldn't put down. Thank you for believing in my vision and for guiding this project with care and kindness.

To my friends—too many to name, but each of you holds a special place in my heart. From Tajikistan to Kazakhstan, Russia to Ukraine, Norway to Sweden, the USA to China, Israel to Singapore to New Zealand, you have brought color and richness to my life. Your impact will stay with me forever. Thank you.